MW01200969

Balanced:

Finding Center as a Work-at-Home Mom

Tricia Goyer

GoyerInk

Balanced: Finding Center as a Work-at-Home Mom

Endorsements

"In the vulnerable moments between tending a child's bad dream and slipping into another hour of much-needed sleep myself, the question has haunted me: 'Is it OK to pursue my passions in the season of motherhood?' Tricia's book is the answer. Not only does she give dozens of examples of how pursuing our God-given passions actually enhances our family life, but she also gifts us with practical wisdom gleaned from years of experience in pursuing her passions. A weight lifted off my chest when I read the list of things Tricia doesn't do, and I was filled with excitement as I caught a glimpse of what life could look like when I embrace fully God's calling and trust the results to Him."
— Trina Holden, blogger at www.TrinaHolden.com and author of Embracing Beauty

"Tricia Goyer's Balanced was the book I had been yearning for and didn't even know it. As a work-at-home mom who is currently struggling to juggle both full-time writing and full-time motherhood to two toddlers and a preschooler, Tricia's message seemed God-ordained for me. This book will bless many, many women by breaking through the guilt and giving work-at-home moms hope that they can fulfill both their professional callings and role of homemaker and mom."

—Erin Odom, owner and creator of The Humbled Homemaker and co-owner of Ultimate Bundles

"If you're a work-from-home mom, I highly recommend Tricia Goyer's eBook, Balanced. Filled with encouragement and practical tips, Tricia draws readers in with her honest, relatable writing. It's comforting to read how another mom juggles work deadlines, family, homeschooling, and chores. She vividly and honestly describes her life and helped me realize I'm not alone in my challenges.

"As a bonus for writers, she explains—and gives great advice on—how she became a writer, as well as how she deals with deadlines and her creative process. The book isn't just for aspiring writers, though; it's beneficial to any mother who wants to work from home."

—Hilary Kimes Bernstein of Accidentally Green and Intentional Stewardship

"As a wife, mother of three preschoolers and one on the way, blogger at Beauty in the Mess, and writer, I have really struggled with balance in my life lately. There have been more days than not that Mommy Guilt hits me as I'm putting the kids to bed at night. It's then that I realize most of the day was spent with my face glued to the computer screen than playing with cars in the living room, cuddling on the couch reading a story, or playing pirates and princesses. Even on days I vow not to let that happen, it just takes one email or one brief look at social media to suck me in. I don't want to miss these little years, as hard as they are at times, just because I'm doing what the Lord has called me to do.

"Balanced was just what this mama needed. Tricia helped me get to the heart of the matter. This is not a 'follow this formula to achieve balance in your life' type book. It's better. While reading the book, I felt like I was having coffee with a mentor and she was helping me navigate exactly what I'm going through with three littles at home while trying to write. Tricia, thank you for sharing your heart, your passion, and helping me see what really matters."

—Whitney Cornelison, blogger at Beauty in the Mess

Table of Contents

Introduction

I've been asked to write this book for years. Work-at-home moms want to know how I host a weekly radio podcast while also homeschooling, raising kids, caring for my husband, and mentoring teenage moms. They want to know how they can do it too—how they can discover God's purpose for their lives. How they can take steps of faith toward the dreams God placed in their hearts, while also loving on the children God's given them.

Writing this book has taken me awhile to get around to for a few reasons. First, I've written a lot. I write four to five books a year, which is a hefty amount for any published writer. Oh yes, and the second reason why it's taken me so long to write this book is because we've been busy filling our home with little ones. In the last three years we've adopted three kids—both through private adoption and adoption through the foster care system. These kids bring the current total of Goyer children to six. I haven't been able to share how I've been able to do it all because I've been trying to balance all of these areas, and I just couldn't find the slot for this book! (Focusing on priorities and saying no to everything else is indeed something I'll be talking about within these pages. Stay tuned!)

Yet, I have to admit there's another reason I haven't dug into this "Balance" project that has been hovering around my heart for a while. The truth is, I feel unbalanced many days. I have a hard time giving advice because I haven't arrived yet. I haven't come to that dreamed-about spot in my work-at-home-ness where I have the perfect schedule and the perfect priorities. I keep thinking one day I'll get my bedroom closet organized, my writing projects organized, and my kids organized, and then I can bestow my wisdom on all of you. Hmm . . . after a few years of striving it hasn't really happened, and the truth is it never will.

That's the beauty of this book. I haven't been able to figure out the perfect balance. I don't always have my act together or even behave nicely. (Just ask my husband and older kids how crazy I get a few days before a book deadline!) Yet even in the midst of my imperfection God uses me. He uses me to write stories for readers and to share ideas with them. He uses me to affirm and assist my husband in his endeavors. He uses me to parent six children at various ages and stages, including homeschooling the younger ones, which some days is a scary thought!

Add to that, God uses me to lead a support group of teenage mothers in inner-city Little Rock, Arkansas. I'm there almost every week encouraging them, "You can do it. Look what God has done for me. God has dreams for you too. God has dreams for your children."

God wants to do the same for you. Not in a perfect way, but in a real one. After all, you're dealing with your own "real life," and hopefully in the midst of it you can find   a little bit of hope, help, and inspiration. Ready to get started?

Confession Time

Yeah! Many, many times I've been in the writing flow and I've patiently stopped to turn my attention to a kiddo who needed me.

Fail! Many times I've been really grumpy when I've had to put my work aside. After all, the work gets far more kudos and acclaim than playing Matchbox cars.

Yeah! On most nights I manage to make dinner, and we eat around the table as a family.

Fail! I'm really bad about procrastinating, and the closer it gets to my book deadlines my family is left to fend for themselves or we get fast food.

Yeah! One thing I'm known for is connecting online with readers. I love Facebook, Twitter, and blogging.

Fail! Sometimes—most of the time?!—it's easier to connect with online readers and friends than the ones who live with me. Taking time to go out to lunch with a friend is hard. It means getting dressed, putting on makeup, and setting aside my writing work for a big chunk of the day.

Pause and Reflect

What about you? Before you read any further, write your own Yeah! and Fail! list.

What things are you doing right?

What things do you need to work on? My guess is that you already know where you need help. You might even know some of the things that will help you.

Ready? Let's go!

I want to warn you: This isn't a simple self-help book. I'm a follower of Jesus Christ. Everything in my life stems from that. I can only do what I do because of Him, so the things I'm going to share start there.

I can give you tips for cleaning off your desk, but from experience I know that change will only come when you clean out the lies, worries, guilt, and fear from not doing enough—not being enough. Worries that stick to your heart like sludge inside the drain in your kitchen sink.

Yes, I will give you tips on how to be balanced in work- at-home parenting and ministry-minded living. But most of what I share here is centered on God's Word because nothing in your life will be balanced unless Jesus is the core of who you are and you allow Him to clean out the center for Himself.

Disclaimer.

This book may not be for you if: You are looking for a simple how-to manual with only schedules, outlines, and agendas. You don't think your spiritual life impacts your work and home life. You think the whole balance issue depends on you and not on your dependence on God.

In this book, there is as much inner work I'm going to talk about as there are ideas, helps, and tips for balancing. Because as someone who's been working at home nearly all of my twenty-four years as a parent, I've discovered three main things:

1. What I do isn't as important as who I am.

2. What God can do in my life and what He's capable of doing can be two very different things—I don't want to limit Him.

3. My outward goals are only reachable if I submit my inward soul to God.

If this sounds like a book you need, good. If not, I understand! We moms only have so much time. You need to spend your time, energy, and hard-earned money on a book that will meet your expectations. Know that I'm praying God will speak to your heart through my story. I hope you'll discover good advice to help you follow the dreams God has placed in your heart and be the wife and mom you've always wanted to be.

Oh, and one more thing. In these pages I talk about my job as a writer. That's what I do. That's what I know. If you work at home in any other job that's not writing I believe you'll still find great advice here. If you are a virtual assistant or an artist, or if you run a catering business, you'll most likely face the same dilemmas I've faced as a work-at-home writing mom. After all, no matter what your job is, you should strive to be professional and do a good job for someone else, while also care for those closest to you.

It can be done, I promise—not perfectly, but well. The most important thing to remember is that God can help you in all areas of your life. He wants to help you. Are you ready to discover how to allow Him to do just that? Let's get started!

Chapter One

My Story of Finding Balance {And Some Practical Starter Ideas}

My journey of being a work-at-home mom started when I was twenty-two years old and pregnant with my third baby. A former teen mom, I'd never considered being an author until a friend from church told me she was working on a novel. I loved reading and writing. Was this something I could do professionally while also staying home and taking care of my kids? I hoped it was.

I started by reading books about writing. I clearly remember reading Writer to Writer by Brock and Bodie Thoene. The encouragement I found in that book really made me believe this was something I could do. Then I had an opportunity to attend the Mount Hermon Christian Writers Conference. I attended with great expectations of finding publishing success. I was sure the year would birth not only a new child but a new career as well. The child came a week early, but the career took much longer. But I didn't give up.

Sometimes I woke before the kids to write. Other times I wrote while they napped. I wrote about things happening in my life. Although only one short article was published during the next three years, I learned a lot—mostly that I could balance writing and kids. All it took was motivation and a little time management. (Yes, prayer helped too!)

After my third year of writing, things really picked up. In the next year I had thirty articles published in national publications such as HomeLife Magazine and Today's Christian Parent. This publishing success meant working with editors and meeting deadlines. It was rewarding to see my name in print, and I felt appreciated by the editors I worked for.

Soon, instead of me sending them ideas, they were contacting me with assignments. This was a big deal for a stay-at-home mom without a college degree. I was thankful I was able to share information and ideas with readers, impacting people I'd never meet in person. I felt God was redeeming all the bad choices I made in high school, and I mostly liked sharing how He was impacting my everyday role as a young mom of three kids.

But I also felt guilty for following my dreams. I homeschooled in the morning, and then in the afternoon I'd set aside a few hours to write while my children played. Those early years, I wrote articles and ideas for novels as Barney played on the television. At least a dozen times during those two hours my kids would ask me for milk, for a snack, or to play with them.

I'd offer what I could but then remind them, "This is Mom's writing time." Guilt weighed me down, and I was sure I was the worst homeschooling mother ever. Other moms seemed completely devoted to their children. They seemed happy playing with their kids, baking, going on long walks, and providing organic meals.

To combat my guilt over taking time to write, I became overcommitted in my parenting, making frequent library trips and signing up my daughter for dance lessons and my boys for sports. I remember days when I'd be exhausted and extremely cranky as I shuttled my children from one practice to another. We were in the car more than at home. And I always seemed to be late. It was hard enjoying soccer practice when I knew I had an article due the next day. And any meltdown that my children had I'd soon join them!

My husband came home from work one day and found me in the kitchen in tears. Bags of groceries were piled on the counters—dinner wasn't close to getting started. The kids were fighting and screaming, and I was near collapse. "I . . . can't . . . do . . . this," I said through blubbering tears. "It's all just too much."

I knew that deep down I was trying to prove myself. Even though I'd never confessed it out loud, I wanted to show others I hadn't messed up my whole life by getting pregnant as a teenager. And the truth is that writing was so much easier than parenting. The words stayed where I put them, and did what I said on the page. The words didn't talk back or throw themselves on the floor. I enjoyed quiet time writing, and then I felt even more guilty for liking it so much. To combat that, I'd add "just one more thing" in our schedules—things to ease my conscience and prove my life wasn't all about writing.

I also went to God time and time again. I prayed for Him to "bring my heart home." I wanted to love parenting more than writing, and I wanted to make it a priority. But forcing it to become a priority turned our lives into a three-ring-circus, with me performing a juggling act and walking a tightrope at the same time.

My husband was the one who urged me to stop the madness. He lovingly told me I didn't have to do it all. I didn't have to keep up with our neighbors and friends. Our kids didn't have to be a part of everything. I didn't have to tackle more writing projects than I felt comfortable with just to prove myself.

I still haven't mastered the juggling and the tightrope walking, but I've made great strides in not tackling both at the same time. It all started with John and me sitting down to figure out our priorities. We asked ourselves a few questions:

What do we want to achieve as a family?
What will matter five years from now—ten years from now? What will mold our children into God-serving adults?
What will bring peace—not stress—to our home?

Here is the list we came up with. This is a list above and beyond the typical things you might expect (such as raising godly children, having a strong marriage, and growing in our personal relationships with God). This practical list helped us to be able to say "yes" or "no" to opportunities that presented themselves. We didn't have to fret over every decision because by following this list, most of the questions of what to sign up for or participate in became clear.

Here is the list:

To provide a godly, homeschooling education for our kids To sign up each child for only one extra-curricular activity a year so we could have more time together

To have dinner as a family to build our family bond

To train our children how to be part of the family unit and do chores

To connect and serve in our local church

To have reading time together as a family at night

To see what God was doing in our lives and follow Him .

Figuring out our priorities helped us set our schedule. Should we sign our son up for soccer? No, because he already played basketball this year. Should we limit television- watching in the evening? Yes, because our priorities are face-to-face dinner, chores, and reading time. Should we help start a children's ministry at our church? Yes, because it's a way for our family to serve together.

We also added the seventh point because we didn't want to be so rigid in our schedule that we couldn't follow God's Spirit. So when opportunities came up to start a teen mom support group or take a mission trip and we felt drawn by God, we could agree as a family on the commitment, even though it was out of the range of 1-6.

I also stopped feeling so guilty. I knew I was focusing on what was most important while letting other "good" things slide. Our life became more centered and peaceful. That's not to say I never felt overwhelmed and overcommitted again, but when I did I knew where to look to discover peace once again.

What about you? Are you trying to do too much, overwhelming yourself and your family with busyness overload?

What are the things that matter most to you? What would your priority list be? I encourage you to answer the questions below.

Pause and Reflect

Think about your family ten years from now. Where do you want to be?

What do you want to accomplish?

What values and godly qualities do you want to embrace? What daily rituals do you want to be part of your life?

Putting Priorities to Work

Once you know your priorities, the next step is to allow them to work for you. It's finding practical ways to live out what matters most to your soul. Maybe you need to cut back on commitments. Maybe you need to write family dinners into your calendar as a daily to-do task. Maybe you need to ask your spouse to give you insight and advice. Taking one positive step after another will lead you to living as you believe.

But, of course, the very first step is always seeking God's wisdom. He knows the present and can see the future. His input on what your priorities should be matters most. But remember that just because God calls you and your family a certain direction doesn't mean you'll never have a struggle as you follow His path. He directs us, then He walks beside us. He doesn't point us in a direction and then ask us to tackle it alone. He asks us to tackle it with Him and be willing to give up our ideals for His steady presence.

Being a work-at-home parent means things WILL have to be sacrificed. You won't be able to do everything other parents do. Your work life will look different. Your family life will look different, but that's OK.

Too often we compare our weaknesses with other people's strengths, only to find ourselves coming up short. What truly matters is simply lifting our faces to heaven and asking, "Lord, what do you think? How do my work, my family, and my priorities look to you?"

If you're on the right track, peace will come. And I don't mean the kind of peace that includes quiet contemplation. (Don't we wish!) But peace that we're loving and serving others the best we can and focusing on the things that truly matter with God's guidance.

Tips from the Trenches

When it comes to working at home, serving in our church and community, and loving our family, we all strive for the same thing: balance. We believe it's out there, and if we discover the right formula we'll finally arrive. There we will have a life that runs with ease—we'll feel "balanced."

Balance is not possible—at least not in the form of a perfect schedule or a perfect routine. Even if we find balance one day, it most likely will slip between our fingers the next. People have unique needs on a daily basis. Work schedules are dependent on other variables. Health wavers, moods change. Husbands have crises at work. The people around us have struggles. Life is a constant shifting.

The only thing we can be certain of is that as soon as we achieve a small measure of balance, something is going to overturn the applecart so all our good intentions will spill out like crabapples, becoming scattered and bruised.

Another truth about balance is that the only One who can control tomorrow (or even the rest of today) is the One who can also provide for our moment-by-moment needs when our schedule gets out of whack. God not only knows what's coming, but He also knows what we need to do today to prepare for it.

How do I work toward balance in my life? Here are a few ways:

1. Schedule naps, dinner, and bedtime. This is a biggie for me! My little kids (six, three, and three) take a nap every day around the same time. We also try to have dinner as a family every night. And we strive to have the kids in bed by 7:30 p.m. Schedules give our children a sense of order. And when I know they'll be in bed at a decent hour, I can look forward to some element of peace in the evening.

2. Pick two or three important things to get done each day. There are days I need to write 2,000 words. There are days I need to get caught up on laundry.

These two things cannot happen on the same day. When I choose what to focus on, I'm also choosing what to ignore. This is important. There will never be enough time to do it all. Ever.

3. Set aside times for fun and play. I give attention to my little ones first thing in the morning instead of jumping onto the computer. I also try to spend an hour of dedicated time with them in the afternoons between the time they wake up from naps and the time I start on dinner. We play in the yard, blow bubbles, or take a walk. When my kids know they'll have dedicated time, they don't have to fight for time (or act up) to try to get it throughout the day.

4. Seek help. I've managed my workload so I can have a young mom come in four hours a week to clean my house. I have assistants who help with my blogs and other online tasks. I have a babysitter who watches my little ones for blocks of time a few times a week so I can write. I was not at this place ten years ago, but I've worked to find people whom I can help financially and who can help me. While you may not be at the place to hire someone, ask yourself if there

is a friend you can trade with. For years I traded homeschool days with another mom—I'd teach her kids for a day and she'd teach mine another—so I'd have a free day. Also, when you see someone who is seemingly "doing it all," that person probably has help, too. No one can do it all and balance everything well. No one.

5. Turn to God. He has the answers for your day. His Spirit will guide you to what's most important. God has good plans for you and your family. Instead of looking to find the perfect schedule—the perfect balance—look to God for His plan for your day. Take your eyes off of that printed-up schedule and put them on Him. He will help you have a healthy and happy family and a productive work life too!

Final Thoughts

"If we take an honest look at a day with our children, we can see that the amount of unconditional attention we give them is minimal. Think about all the things you do with and for your children. From this mental list, remove all the things that you feel you have to do (as part of your responsibilities as a parent or grandparent), all the things you do out of guilt because you think you fell short of your obligations, and all the time spent reminding or disciplining your children. How much time is left for the sheer enjoyment of each other? How many interactions are truly unconditional? If you are like me, those moments occur when the child is sleeping. We gaze at our sleeping little ones, overflowing with love for them. What we feel when they wake up and dawdle getting dressed, however, is a different matter."[1]

Chapter Two
How Your Work Benefits from You
Being at Home

Recently my husband got a new job, and one of things we both were excited about was the benefits package. The benefits included health insurance, dental insurance, vision care, and so much more. Considering my benefits from working at home made me chuckle: working in my pajamas, access to a number of break rooms (sometimes nap rooms), Thomas the Tank Engine as background music, and toddler kisses. I could go on and on about the benefits, but I've also discovered my work benefits from me being at home, too.

When is the last time, as a work-at-home mom, that you sat all day and just worked? Is it even possible? We fix meals, change diapers, say no a hundred times a day (and many yes's too), and give lots of hugs. As we live in the real world we discover priorities and real-life issues. As a writer, it's where I discover stories too.

Early on, my real struggles became the inspiration for articles I wrote. If I was struggling with my kids being picky eaters, teaching them to share, or dealing with a reluctant reader, I figured other parents were, too. Knowing this, I queried magazines and proposed articles about those topics. Then, once the editor said he or she was interested, I'd contact authors or other professionals on parenting to ask their advice. Yes, that's right—I'd get free advice from the pros for the very things I struggled with . . . and then I'd get paid to write about it! How cool is that?

What about you? Can the real struggles of being a mom help your work life? I bet they can. Some of the benefits are obvious: flexible schedules and fewer expenses for child care. There are also no commuting expenses or the added costs of transportation and work clothes. Here are other ways that my work life has benefited from my home life:

1. Working at home put me into the real world of real problems I have to solve. I dealt with kids, neighbors, preschool groups, and people at church. I chatted with other moms about their struggles. I faced struggles of my own. This real-life training made me flexible and knowledgeable. I learned how to solve problems, big and small. After all, if I could be patient with a cranky toddler, I also knew how to be patient with a cranky editor or reader. (Thankfully those are few and far between!)

2. Working at home keeps my emotions on the surface, and I put them to good use in my writing! I've lost my children in shopping centers (well, they wandered off!) and felt the panic of that. I've stayed up late worrying when I knew my teen was driving on icy roads. I've rushed to the emergency room with kids who needed casts and stitches. Those events often don't make it into my novels, but the emotions do. Often the things that happen in my day are the sparks for new ideas that lead to other new ideas that become my books. I'm not sure what well of experience I'd draw from if I spent eight hours

entering data in an office with just me and my computer screen or stuffing my emotions because of conflict with my co-workers that I'd try to brush off as "just business."

3. Working at home taught me how to juggle projects. Tell me the truth—do you ever get to finish one thing before something else comes up? We mothers are used to the art of juggling—running from the grocery store to the laundry room to the park. One kid wants one thing, another needs something else. It seems our very existence as mothers is a juggle! As a writer, too, I have dozens of things happening at once. I have books in the proposal stage, books in the writing stage, and books in the editing stage. I have galleys to read and covers to review. My mind bounces from thing to thing, much like it bounces from cooking to cleaning to chasing kids.

4. Working at home allowed me to serve in my church and community, which became training ground for leadership. As a work-at-home mom I was able to serve during the week when other people were at work, and these service opportunities have become

an unexpected training ground. It started out by being asked to volunteer at vacation Bible school or filling in to help with a mid-week Bible study. Each little step taught me about influencing others, directing projects, and helping people. As the avenues to serve grew, my leadership skills grew, too. For example, leading a Bible study and working with others in MOPS (Mothers of Preschoolers) showed me that I could help women and that God had a calling on my life to connect with them not only through my writing but face to face. These simple acts of outreach planted seeds to what later took root and bloomed as speaking and radio ministries! People were people, I discovered, and I had a few things to say that could encourage them.

5. Working at home provided a crash course in time management. When I first started homeschooling my three oldest kids (ages six, three, and one) in 1995, I thought my life from that moment would always be about homeschooling. I pictured all of my time, or at least most of it, shaping my children's education. I scheduled my day in fifteen-

minute increments and did my best to stick to it. If I wanted to get anything done beyond homeschooling I had to be diligent about focusing on priorities, making lists, and setting goals. Eventually I realized that scheduling life or work in fifteen-minute increments was an exercise in futility. Life and work don't always run on schedule; instead I've learned to focus on cutting out time wasters so I take care of my priorities. (More to come on those time wasters!)

6. Working at home helped me be more productive. When I sit down at the computer I only have a few hours at a time to write (if that!)—so I have to get things done. I can't play Solitaire or Candy Crush, or whatever the latest craze is. When I know I only have thirty minutes to work, I don't dawdle. I focus. This get-to-it-ness helped me as my career progressed. And yes, it has progressed.

7. Working at home has made me more prayerful. Both my work life and my home life bring me to my knees. I can't parent without God. I can't write without God. I can't be a wife, friend, or minister to teen mothers without Him.

8. Working at home allowed me to focus on God as my Boss. Colossians 3:23-24 says, "Whatever you do, work heartily, as for the Lord and not for men, knowing that from the Lord you will receive the inheritance as your reward. You are serving the Lord Christ" (ESV). We are all called to work as if God is our boss, yet that can seem hard when there's a flesh-and-bones person telling you what to do. But working from home has made this very real for me. During my early work-at-home years I learned to listen to God's voice to discern what projects I should pursue. After all, I only had so much time. Yet as I saw God work in small ways, I began to trust Him in bigger ways. I figured He loved me and my kids more than anyone. He knew the future and where He wanted to take my work. Why shouldn't I trust that? In each of these ways I became a better employee in a world of kids and chaos. That is the definition of true success!

Pause and Reflect

What are some benefits from working at home that you've experienced (or that you hope to experience)? In what ways does being a mom make you a better employee? How have you learned leadership in your role as a mom?

Picture your home life and work life five years from now; how will each have changed?

Tips from the Trenches

On this journey of balance, of working, and of serving, you will be overwhelmed. There will be times that you have a work project due the next day and you're finally able to turn your attention to it at 9:00 p.m. when you're exhausted, your head pounds, and you'd rather watch mindless television, people-creep on Facebook, or just go to bed. I know. I've been there. I've been there more times than I can count. I was just there last week. I was opening up a document to work on and I literally thought, "I'd rather be scrubbing toilets or picking up a carpet full of tiny Lego pieces right now than working on this." There's only one thing that helps at times like that, and that's to pray.

Pray for wisdom. Pray for strength. Pray for diligence.
Pray against temptation to creep over to Facebook.
Pray for the words.
Pray for the message. Pray for favor.
Pray for speediness at work.

And later, when I get kudos from my editor/boss, or I read a great review on Amazon.com, I can turn that praise over to God. I know that if it were up to me, I'd have given up. I know the words didn't percolate in my brain because I went to a beach, sat on the warm sand with a journal, and fed my creative soul. If I would have waited for my creative soul to be filled up, I might have been able to finish one book in twelve years rather than forty books.

I can't tell you the number of times I've bribed myself with this: "You can check Facebook/email/last night's red carpet gowns after you write 1,000 words and no less." And I do it. I write these words even when I'm exhausted. Why? Not because I'm super talented or super disciplined, but because I pray.

Friend, do you hear the Lord God speaking to your heart right now? Read these words from Isaiah 48:17: "I am the LORD your God, who teaches you what is best for you, who directs you in the way you should go" (NIV).

Or the TG (Tricia Goyer) expanded translation: "I will sit next to you and remind you to focus on your work, rather than the internet. I will give you the words when you are dead tired and have Mom-brain. I won't leave you hanging when all your friends are at a Girls' Night Out and you're burning the midnight oil on your computer. I will be there, and I will see you. More than that, your love and dedication—as tiny as it may seem at that time—will thrill me, and I will pour into you more than you expect. People's lives will be impacted by you more than you know because of me. Through your faithfulness, I can be glorified in ways that wouldn't come otherwise. For my glory."

That's beautiful, isn't it? And it's truth. BUT I would not be doing you any favors if I were to end the chapter here. It's good to talk about the flip side as well. Just because you want to do something and you pray about it doesn't mean God will endorse your project. I can't count the number of hours I've poured time, attention, and prayer into something just to have it drop like a boulder to the bottom of the sea and go nowhere.

This happens when I'm looking at the marketplace or at my own ego instead of looking to God. Occasionally the idea is right, but the timing isn't. Or the message is right but spiritually and emotionally I'm not at the best place to share it. God knows us better than we know ourselves. So if there is a project you're focusing on, pouring yourself into, and hitting your head against the wall because of rejection, release that to God, too. And know that coming to that place of humble relinquishment just might be the best benefit of all.

Final Thoughts

Vision is knowing where you want to head and having an idea of how to get there. Prayerful vision is asking God to show you what He sees since He has a much higher, better view than we do, and adjusting your heart to His desires for your work, your family, and His world.

Chapter Three
How My Kids Benefit from My Work-at-Home-Ness

I'm a mom by day, writer by night . . . and I don't write just anything—I write novels of suspense and danger, epic events, uncommon characters, and romance. You would think someone who writes about things like that would have a suspenseful, dangerous, uncommon life. That's not the case, although I do have an amazing husband who assists in the romance department!

Living in these two worlds is strange. I'm torn between the imagined, "ship-sinking, love-confessing, truth- revealing world" and the real-life, "macaroni-and-cheese, kids'-television, and diaper-changing world." Sometimes they happen at the same time. I confess to writing dramatic scenes to strains of Dora the Explorer's "I'm a map, I'm a map, I'm a map, I'm a map!"

The truth is that my three little kids have no idea their mom writes books. I read books, yes. Farmyard tales and nursery rhymes are their favorites. I color in coloring books with them, and I try to keep them from coloring in my books . . . but to our three youngest kids, Alyssa, Bella, and Casey, I'm just Mom. I'm also "just mom" to my three older kids. They think it's cool when I get a new book published, but it's about as cool as getting chicken and mashed potatoes for dinner!

The wonderful thing about following my dreams during the hands-on mothering years is that I started seeing my dreams come true. I got articles published, then books.   I started speaking for groups and conferences. Soon I was being interviewed on radio and television shows. Sometimes I even traveled for research, visiting amazing places.

And you know what? My kids were with me along the way. They saw me work hard, but they also saw the results— and they often got to enjoy the results. They learned dreams were achievable, and they saw the real ways I went about to make them happen.

Dreams don't happen if they stay dreams; you have to do something about them.

Here are just a few ways my kids have benefited from my work:

1. My kids have had their lives chronicled. My older kids enjoy reading about themselves in my articles and blogs. Because I'm always looking for the next life story to share, I'm uber-aware of the life happening around us. I talk about everyday moments that would otherwise be lost in ordinary, daily busyness. Of course, I also ask permission to share their stories. For the most part I've been given go-aheads. As for the stories my kids don't want me to share, I respect their wishes and keep my mouth sealed and my fingers stilled.

2. My kids get proud of having an author mom—it boosts their family identity. They sometimes take my books to church to show their friends. My older kids have gained the attention (and extra interest) from their college professors when they discover my occupation.

3. My kids have traveled to amazing places on vacation/research trips. Vancouver, Canada, St. Louis, Seattle, and California are just a few of the places where they and my husband have joined me on business trips. (And after a little business, we had a lot of fun!)

4. My kids have met amazing people I connect with in my work: missionaries, fellow authors, models, World War II veterans, and even popular musicians. In fact, the day they first told me having a mom as a writer was cool was when I was able to get us free tickets and backstage passes to see the Newsboys. (I remind them of my coolness when I'm under deadline and bring home Taco Bell yet again.)

5. My kids have a more compassionate and understanding mom. Writing books has changed me inside. While researching many of my non- fiction titles and hearing about the hardships people face, I've become more compassionate. When I wrote about the Holocaust in my fiction, I realized even more what was really important in life—family and

faith. When I recently wrote about the Titanic, I hugged my toddler tighter before I put her to bed.

6. I'm always checking to see if I'm measuring up to the "writer mom" I'm claiming to be in the books and blogs I write. I tell my husband often, "I want to live the type of life I like to write about." Because of this, I live better so I can write better and still be truthful and real.

7. My kids have seen me model what it means to follow one's dreams. They've witnessed me listening to God's call, setting goals, and putting my rear in the chair to work. My example has fostered inside them a longing to discover God's dreams for their own lives. In fact as I write this, my twenty- one-year-old daughter is living in Europe for a year— on her own—as a missionary, and both of my older boys, ages twenty-four and nineteen, are working on novels. Our kids follow not what we tell them but what they see modeled in us. This doesn't just mean they follow how I treat the dog or what I say about the neighbors when they're out of earshot, although that's important too. My older kids are picking up on

my passion, my mission, and my dedication even when I don't think they're looking. It's God's version of making disciples in pint-sized packages. I can't wait to see what God has in store for these kids! Yes, God's dreams and the work He has called me to do are for my benefit, the world's benefit, and my kids' benefit too!

So is it worth it to follow your dreams and to spend time working on something you're passionate about while raising kids? It has been for me. If you ask my kids, I'd bet they'll tell you it's been worth it to them, too, but you have to track them down first. As they've grown older, they're not around as much. They're living out their dreams, following their hearts' pursuits. They didn't get that from me nagging them; they learned it from seeing me struggle and strive, and that has been the best result. I created a family of dream-seekers and didn't even realize I was doing it. Another dream fulfilled!

Pause and Reflect

How can your kids benefit from you working at home? Write down as many possibilities as you can list.

Places we can travel:

Experiences we can have:

People we can meet:

Changes in our standard of living:

Attitudes and values developed:

It's often easy to point out what our kids lose by our work, especially our time and attention, but look at all they can gain!

Kids Learn What They See

I want to expound on my last point about being a model for our kids because it's important. I've had to have an attitude adjustment about my expectations. Through the years I've noticed society puts a lot of pressure on us moms, and often we buy into their thinking that our children need to be the center of our world. I love my children. I strive to be a good mom, but running a child-centered home doesn't do anyone any good . . . especially my kids! Instead, children need to be seen as a welcome part of our family and home but not the focus of it.

Until the last hundred years children spent the majority of their time with their parents. Young girls were in the home, learning how to be a household manager who would care for and keep her own home someday. Boys were often with their dads, learning a trade or tending the fields. When you spend a lot of time together, kids follow what they see. They also ask questions. A lot of questions.

"What are you doing? Why are you doing that? What are you working on? When are you going to be done?"

These questions can be annoying, but it helps to remember they can be the very things that guide our children to their own work and service for God and others someday. I love this passage from Joshua 4:1-7 (NLT) that talks about this:

When all the people had crossed the Jordan, the LORD said to Joshua, "Now choose twelve men, one from each tribe. Tell them, 'Take twelve stones from the very place where the priests are standing in the middle of the Jordan. Carry them out and pile them up at the place where you will camp tonight.'" So Joshua called together the twelve men he had chosen—one from each of the tribes of Israel. He told them, "Go into the middle of the Jordan, in front of the Ark of the Lord your God. Each of you must pick up one stone and carry it out on your shoulder— twelve stones in all, one for each of the twelve tribes of Israel. We will use these stones to build a memorial. In the future your children will ask you, 'What do these stones mean?' Then you can tell them, 'They remind us that the Jordan River stopped flowing when the Ark of the Lord's Covenant went across.' These stones will stand as a memorial among the people of Israel forever."

God had the Israelites build a memorial so future generations would ask about it—and in their asking they would hear about the great deeds of God. Daily we are building memorials. When our children see the work of our hands they will ask questions. (We want them to ask questions!)

We do the best job at teaching our children about the activity of God in our work and life when our children see the activity—when they see God at work. Yes, taking our children to Bible study and church so they can learn from other godly people is important. But the biggest impact in their lives will come from watching us and seeing how God works in ordinary lives in ordinary ways. This can truly be an amazing training ground for your kids in the things that really matter—the eternal things!

Three More Benefits for the Writer-Mamas Among You

Writing teaches our kids there is a world that God wants us to impact with the Good News.

Writing hones our messages. It helps us process life.

Time spent writing teaches our kids about our unique callings, our dependence on Jesus, and our dedication to sharing Him with the world.

Final Thoughts:

Saying, "Do what I say, not what I do," never works for kids. They have to see it to believe it!

Define the things that matter most to you.

Now, consider how you can show your kids these things are important.

Chapter Four

What Does God Have In Mind When

He Selects and Shapes a Person?

The truth is that you have the skills, talents, and desires you do because God has gifted these things to you. Not everyone has the ability to balance both being a mom and working at home. It's a very special club. It's also a huge challenge. It's hard enough managing one of these worlds, but managing and melding the two is nearly impossible.

Yet knowing this takes the pressure off of you, in a way. Since you can't depend on your own skills, talents, and desires in the distinct worlds of working and being a mom, it will force you to turn to God. The greater the challenges, the greater your dependence on Him. And that is exactly where we all need to be!

Take a moment and picture yourself as a lump of clay sitting on a potter's wheel. Imagine God taking that lump and forming it into a serving vessel. It's a unique vessel that can be used in numerous ways and on different occasions. Yet the vessel cannot move on its own. More accurately, it cannot move unless Someone moves it. Picture God leaning down from heaven and breathing life into that jar of clay. And then picture putting yourself into His hands to be used in various ways—at His disposal, to serve those He cares for, for His glory.

As we walk through life, we like to think we're in control. We believe we make decisions, but without God we aren't getting anywhere. God talked about this to Moses—a slave, turned prince, turned shepherd, turned leader of Israel.

Then the LORD asked Moses, "Who makes a person's mouth? Who decides whether people speak or do not speak, hear or do not hear, see or do not see? Is it not I, the LORD? Now go! I will be with you as you speak, and I will instruct you in what to say," Exodus 4:11-12 (NLT).

You see, it's His job to take you and use you just as He used Moses. And He used Moses in some pretty powerful ways! But Moses couldn't do it on his own and neither can we.

As I mentioned before, I started writing in 1994 when I was twenty-two years old and pregnant with my third child. But the call came before that in 1992. From the very first moment I sat down to follow this calling I've been trying to figure out the balance between writing and taking care of my family. Did you catch that word: calling? I have no doubt I was called to write. When my friend Cindy Martinusen Coloma told me she was working on a novel, something stirred within me. I knew at that moment I wanted to write. Why hadn't I thought of it before? I had grown up loving to read, but the idea of becoming a writer hadn't crossed my mind. Once it did, the desire never swayed.

It's strange when I think of that now. In the last twenty- something years I cannot remember a time when I didn't see writing in my future.

Do you feel called to your work? If so, do you remember the moment God called you to it? What did you feel? Fear? Excitement? Both?

Writing is hard enough . . . but writing with kids at home takes skill and strategy. Simply siting down and putting insightful and inspirational words on paper with kids running around is impossible. (Yes, you can no doubt get something on the paper, but odds are it won't be insightful or inspiring!)

I first started writing during my kids' nap time. John and I lived in low-income housing while he went to college. The whole apartment was 600 square feet, and there was a tiny desk in the very small corner of the living room.

Thinking back on that time, I now realize God was equipping and empowering me to achieve His purpose. I had no idea whom He was growing me to be. I didn't know the books and articles He would bloom from my heart. I just knew I got excited as I sat down at my computer. I had this inner stirring that my work was worth spending nap time on.

I couldn't have known the messages and ministries to come. I had no idea future things like blogs, or Facebook, or Twitter were on the horizon, or that I'd be able to reach tens of thousands of people daily with the good news of Jesus through these social media outlets. But God knew.

And He placed the desire on my heart to do something, even though that something didn't look like it was doing much of anything since I was getting a lot of rejections. What I didn't realize was that I was in training so I'd be ready for publication. I was learning how to balance work and family. I was learning to set priorities.

Maybe you're trying to figure out how to meet deadline- focused work contracts, or maybe you're just trying to spend thirty minutes a day on something important that stirs within. To God, your faithfulness is what matters most. Your faithfulness to the work is more important than the outcome. Honestly! When we do the work He's called us to do, we can trust the outcome to Him.

I love this verse I found just the other day: "Every GOD-direction is road tested," Psalm 18:30 (The Message). God is better than any GPS. He not only takes you where you need to go, He also knows what's waiting ahead. And if you allow Him, He will prepare you for the journey to come.

Yes, God will empower you to achieve His purpose. He will enable you to influence more lives than you can ever imagine, in ways you can't even start to picture. And He will help you start at home! God gave me a motto a while ago: "I want to live the type of life I can write about." What good is writing about raising godly kids if you're not actually doing it? What good is inspiring others out there to serve God will all their heart if you're not spending time doing it with your kids? What good is making enough money to take your family on nice vacations if you're robbing them of quality time at home?

We don't need just to be great employees—we need be great parents first. And as we do that, we'll be able to step fully into the work God has called us to do beyond our front doors or on the other side of the computer screen!

At no other time in history have ordinary women, from the comfort of our homes, been able to impact so many for the kingdom of God while at the same time overseeing the shaping of little souls. How amazing is that?

God has a plan for both aspects of our lives! The trick is balancing them—not being overwhelmed but trusting God for the outcome. This was something I had to learn, and I'm still learning. It all started with understanding I am a vessel in God's hands. I am His to use as He sees fit, without trying to move on my own power.

Think on This

"Would you rather try to endorse your own ministry before people or would you rather have God endorse and affirm you? You do not confirm your ministry, God does! If He does not, you are in trouble. You can launch a public-relations campaign so you will be more acceptable. However, seeking acceptance from the world is of no use to God. You do not have to announce you are going to have a big building program and then blame the people if it does not work. If God wants a building program, it will work. If you start something and it does not seem to go well, consider carefully that God, on purpose, may not be authenticating what you told the people—because it did not come from Him, but from your own head. You may have wanted to do something outstanding for God and forgot that God does not want that. He wants you to be available to Him, and more important, to be obedient to Him. God is looking for a person in whom He can entrust His leadership. The key is not what a person can do, but what God will do in and through a person's life."2 Henry Blackaby, Chosen to be God's Prophet

Pause and Reflect:

What outstanding things do you want to do for God? Why do you think you want to do those things?

What outstanding things does God want to do through you? How has God confirmed to you that this is His plan?

If He hasn't yet, have you prayed that He'll show you a clear path? Trust Him to direct your paths!

Tips from the Trenches

"Explain what you do to your children as early as you can. Be specific and talk to them in ways they can understand. A two-year-old cannot see that Mom needs to have 90,000 words edited and turned in by next week, but a teenager with homework can understand you have a deadline and need to do certain things to reach it.

"Have a place for them near where you work. Whether you're a kitchen-table writer or have your own office, provide a spot where children can sit and do their own work. It can be a desk, a corner, or whatever. When I had my office, I had a sofa in there. My kids could hang out, read, nap, whatever, and they were with me. It was their space, which made them feel like they weren't banished."

—novelist, Kathleen Y'Barbo-Turner

Before We Go Further...We Have to Talk about Comparing Ourselves to Others

I mentioned before I started my writing journey with my friend Cindy Martinusen Coloma. She was an amazing support to me. We read books on writing together. We talked about ideas. We attended our first writing workshop—and even our first writers conference—together. I don't know why, but I just expected we'd both get our first books published at the same time too.

Cindy and I were both working on novels when I got the call from our mutual agent. I had a book going to publishing committee, which is where publishers decide if they are going to publish a book. And the amazing thing is that Cindy did, too! Yes, the same publishing committee on the same day!

Deep down I knew God was going to do a miracle. I felt that since we'd started on the writing journey together that we'd start on the publishing journey together, too. The day before my birthday, the phone rang. It was my agent. Excited, I totally believed I was going to get an early birthday present. Instead I got the news that Cindy's book was accepted and mine wasn't. I was crushed. I cried for the whole day. I'd made it so close. And even though I was trying to be excited for my friend, I was disappointed and depressed.

Maybe you've been in a similar spot. You've been working so hard at your business. You've given it your all yet, compared to those around you, you feel like you are falling short.

Today, do you feel discouraged? Do you see others having success at all levels and wonder when it will be your turn? You need to remember that you are a special creation, unique and precious to God.

Yet why do we struggle, comparing our lives, our work, our bodies, our kids, and our talents—or lack of talents—with others? I sometimes still do this with my writing. I look at the bestseller list with longing. I consider the big advances and media fan-fare some authors receive, and then I sigh. I do this in other areas too. How come my friend can eat anything she wants and stay slim? Why do I have to exercise hard and watch what I eat just to maintain?"How come?" "What if?" "Why?" "Why not?"

Instead of comparing, we need to look past who we dream to be and consider God's dreams instead.

In God's word, we read, "God-of-the-Angel-Armies speaks: 'Exactly as I planned, it will happen. Following my blueprints, it will take shape'" Isaiah 14:24 (The Message).

The word "planned" here is translated "compare." It's as if God has weighed the different possibilities, looked at them from all angles, and then chosen the best way. He makes the blueprints . . . then He constructs them into our reality.

The life we have is the one constructed for us by an all- loving God. It's not the life, body, health, or circumstances we wish we had. It's not a perfect life we strive to attain but it's the life He means for us. God drew the blueprints. He's the one molding the form, transforming it into reality.

"Remember your history, your long and rich history. I am GOD, the only God you've had or ever will have— incomparable, irreplaceable—from the very beginning telling you what the ending will be, all along letting you in on what is going to happen, assuring you, 'I'm in this for the long haul, I'll do exactly what I set out to do,'" we read in Isaiah 46:8–11 (The Message).

It's OK to have longings. But don't let not reaching your dreams discourage you. Instead we need to realize we are living His dreams. And even the hard stuff, especially the hard stuff, that we face today is preparing us to be the people He has designed us to be.

Hindsight is 20/20, and looking back I can see why God didn't give me that first book contract. I wasn't ready emotionally or professionally as a writer. He also had other things for me to do, including caring for my dying grandfather and helping start a crisis pregnancy center. Today I am thankful God said no then. Knowing this makes me take current rejections with more trust and acceptance. Even though I'm disappointed now, someday I'll understand His reasons. (If not in this life, I'll understand in eternity!) You see, God loves us completely and has perfect plans for us—plans we'd choose if we could love unconditionally and see limitlessly like He does.

God has longings for us even greater than we imagine, and He's willing to tell us these things as we seek Him out. Not seek our dreams, but seek Him . . . and ask Him to plant His dreams in our hearts. Will you seek Him today? Pray. Open your heart. And dare to listen to God's dreams for you. Don't compare. Dare to trust that God's plan is perfect, even when it seems you're getting the short end of the stick. Because I promise His plan is perfect. I promise that deep down He is going to do a miracle, beginning in your heart.

Chapter Five
Working and Serving from Your Core

What makes you do what you do?

I love this mantra that author and speaker Sam Horn replays in her mind every time she gets up to speak: "I am here to serve; not to show off. I am here to inspire; not to impress. I am here to make a difference; not to make a name."3

Think about that mantra for your home, your work, your service to God and your family. Take a few minutes to write out your own mantra. Here is my attempt at that (Maybe you've heard me say this a few times already in this book?):

I want to live the type of life I want to write about. I want to serve others with the love of Jesus pouring through me.

It's a simple goal, but the meaning behind it carries my steps throughout the day. If I'm here to serve, then I'm here to follow the servant-leader attitude of Jesus. He didn't lead with an iron fist but with a gentleness of heart. He knew His followers were weak. He realized they had flaws, and He didn't expect perfection. Yet Jesus still stepped out with a set to His chin, knowing His greatest love would mean giving everything He had . . . all of Himself. Jesus wasn't a show-off. Showing up and following through were most important to Him.

Jesus wasn't there to impress. He had legions of angels at His disposal. He could have given His followers quite the show. Instead, He wanted to inspire them so they'd turn to God.

"Inspiration" means God-breathed. Jesus was God's breath in human form. Jesus was all about God's business. Jesus wasn't out to make a name for Himself. In fact, again and again when He healed, He told people to keep the miracle to themselves.

After healing a man of leprosy, "Jesus sent him away at once with a strong warning: 'See that you don't tell this to anyone,'" Mark 1:43–44a (NIV). Jesus knew that publicity about His miracles would divert attention away from His message. He wanted to make an eternal difference, one He could only do with His sacrifice, not with His healing and deliverance. Those were only temporary fixes, and Jesus knew that much more—men's souls—was at stake.

The truth is that even though you might do some really great work, you might not impress others as much as you think. You may not impress those you work for, and usually the clean house, clean laundry, and healthy dinner won't impress your kids. But this is good news, really! As you work at home, your children keep you humble, grounded, and eternally focused. As you look at their little faces, you can remember daily, hourly, what your true purpose in life is about.

Working at home will remind you that you're not out to make a name for yourself. In fact, "Mom" is the greatest name you can be called, greater than "best-seller," "award- winner," or "top employee." By working at home you're able to make a difference in two arenas—close up and out there. When you inspire others outside of your home, your children will see not only that they aren't the center of the universe but that serving and helping others is something worth working hard for. And as you serve your children in everyday life, you'll be reminded again and again what really matters. The truth is, God is the co-writer in the story of my life and the stories I write. And, well, that makes it downright epic.

Tips from the Trenches

"One tip on mothering and working at home: Don't wait until the optimal time to work. That time will never come. Schedule time to work and stick to that schedule as best you can: with babies at your feet, in your lap, when they're down for a quick nap, or as you're waiting in line for carpool.

"I wrote my first novel when I was a soccer mom of two and working outside the home. I also wrote from ten at night to two in the morning. It took me two years, but I got the novel done! Those late-night hours are still my most productive. Creature of habit, I guess.

"Do I want to write a novel or have a perfectly clean house? If you could see my house now, you'd know the answer to that question. A little dust never hurt anyone, and honestly, it's just going to come right back. You can clean it next week. Or the next."
—Best-selling novelist Tamera Alexander

Think on This

"The best time for planning a book is while you're doing the dishes."
—Agatha Christie

Mom, It's Your Job to Shape Your World

Balance starts with shaping your world. Each of us has a chance to "shape and form" our calendars, our schedules, and even our expectations.

Think about it: What other creature do you know that has the capacity to manage his/her day or plan six months ahead? None. We are different. We are made into the image of God. God formed. God filled. He set a calendar, a schedule, and had expectations of when His work would be completed.

Have you ever noticed this pattern in Scripture? First God formed the spaces . . . and then He filled them.

FORMED: Day one: God created light and formed the heavens and the earth.

FILLED: Day four: He filled the sky with the sun, moon, and stars.

FORMED: Day two: God separated the water and sky. FILLED: Day five: He filled the earth with fish and birds FORMED: Day three: God formed the land and vegetations.

FILLED: Day six: He filled it with animals and man.

Our problem is that we fill before we form. Balance means forming before filling. It means planning what we want the world we're creating to look like, making sure we have our territories, boundaries, and calendar white space in place before we start scheduling in. But how do we do that?

Remember in chapter one when I talked about John and me figuring out our priorities? Here was the list:

1 .   To provide a godly, homeschooling education for our kids

2 .   To sign up each child for only one extra-curricular activity a year so we could have more time together

3 .   To have dinner as a family to build our family bond

4 .   To train our children how to be part of the family unit and do chores

5 .   To connect and serve in our local church

6 .   To have reading time together as a family at night

7 .   To see what God was doing in our lives and follow Him .

Establishing our priorities gave us a guide for what our daily life should look like. Having these priorities also guided us on what NOT to do. For example, because we wanted to have dinner together as a family most nights, I made sure the shopping was done, I set aside my afternoons for cooking dinner, and I limited the amount of activities my kids were involved in so they didn't interfere with that priority.

But life changes, kids grow, and your priorities may change too. Or they may not. Twenty years after writing this list, do you know what my priorities are now?

1 . To provide a godly, homeschooling education for our kids

2 . To sign up each child for one extra-curricular activity a year so we can have more time together

3 . To have dinner time as a family to build our family bond

4 . To train our children how to be part of the family unit and do chores

5 . To connect and serve in our local church

6 . To have reading time together as a family at night

7 .   To see what God was doing in our lives and follow Him .

These priorities have worked well for us, and we're sticking to them!

I'm not saying these should be your priorities. I am saying you need to figure out what your priorities are. Do you want to know how to do that?

Below is a story I shared in my co-written book *Lead Your Family Like Jesus* (Focus on the Family). The first step in figuring out your priorities is cutting out what are not your priorities so you have space for what's most important.

"Most of us spend too much time on what is urgent and not enough time on what is important."
—Stephen R. Covey

How to Form Your Calendar Before You Fill It

{Excerpt from my co-written book Lead Your Family Like Jesus}

My calendar was in chaos. I was having trouble making wise choices about my commitments and my family's activities. One night I broke down crying from being overwhelmed.

My husband, John, asked if we could sit down and go over my schedule. He wanted us to look at everything I'd committed to and figure out where the problem was. He started by asking me to make a list of everything I did in a week.

I scoffed. "You don't have enough paper," I said. Feeling a burden heavy on my shoulders, I started going through the list—caring for our home and children, my work projects, my volunteering, my church service, and all the kids' activities.

After everything was listed, John helped me to rate everything on a scale of one through four. The "ones" were things I had to do, such as feeding the kids and homeschooling. The "twos" were things I should do, like laundry and housecleaning. The "threes" were things I enjoyed doing and that helped me, such as Bible study or exercise class. The fours, I discovered, were things I did because I was afraid to say no, or because I wanted to look good or have my kids look good.

To refocus and get a better handle on my schedule, I cut out all the fours. I even cut out some threes, realizing that even though they were good things, it wasn't the right season for them.

Evaluating my activities helped my schedule, and it gave me a glimpse into my heart. I was trying to get others—even God—to love me because of things I did. I realized, though, that God loves me already. When I focus on Him and His plans for me, I can find peace—and have confidence in the things I choose, knowing I'm doing them for God alone.4

Pause and Reflect

Are you currently volunteering because you didn't want to say no, or did you sign your kids up for an activity because everyone else did? How would you feel if you didn't have

those things on your calendar?

Spend some time going through your schedule. Rank everything 1–4.

1. Things you have to do (feed children, get them dressed, homeschooling/homework, work projects, Bible study, and prayer) .

2. Things you should do (laundry, cook dinner, bathe your kids, serve others, church attendance) .

3. Things you want to do (things you enjoy doing/things that help you: Facebook, Bible study group, exercise class, coffee with a friend, your child's favorite sport or activity) .

4. Things you are doing to look good or are doing out of guilt (volunteering because you couldn't say no, extra extracurricular activities, things that you think will make you a good mom).

• Now, cut out all the 4s .

• Limit the 3s, realizing there will be different seasons in life when you can do them .

• Take a moment to appreciate the white space .

• Pick 5–10 things you want to fill your calendar with: family dinners, church attendance, quiet time with God, your child's favorite sport or class .

• Realize that your choices today will make the days to come—and the years to come—so much easier!

Tips from the Trenches

"Think long-term. What seems more exciting and fulfilling (i.e. writing and being published) will come and go. Motherhood will last for a lifetime. If the goal is to have a healthy, loving, adult relationship with your kids, you must invest in that relationship in their growing-up years. Saying 'yes' to something good may mean you are saying 'no' to something better or even the best!"

—parenting author Kendra Smiley

Even the Pros Agree

"A lot of parents are exhausted by their own over-parenting," said Bryan Caplan, an economics professor at George Mason University. "They make so many sacrifices and are so stressed out by driving around so much that they explode at kids for changing the radio station."

But isn't getting our kids involved in lots of activities for their ultimate good? Not necessarily. Some of the most interesting insights into this question come not from psychologists, but economists.

"It's easy to take a look at the more successful kids and assume that all the activities are why they are more successful," Professor Caplan said. But research doesn't bear that out.

On a recent National Public Radio program, Steven D. Levitt, a professor of economics at the University of Chicago, said he and another economist could find no evidence that that sort of parental choices could be correlated at all with academic success.

"And my guess is," he went on, "that when it comes to the happiness of kids, that kind of cramming has got to be negatively correlated. Being rushed from one event to the other is just not the way most kids want to live their lives, at least not my kid."5

Think on This

"Things which matter most must never be at the mercy of things which matter least."

—German writer Johann Wolfgang von Goethe

Chapter Six

Becoming the Master Architect of Your Own Schedule

I'd like you to pause and think about building construction for a minute. When I lived in Montana one of my favorite things to do was to visit old settlers' cabins. We'd be driving down a country road and out in the field would be a small structure with its wood boards, faded and gray, the roof sagging, and the windows and door missing. Maybe it was the novelist in me, but I always liked to imagine who built that cabin and settled in it. They had dreams. They had hopes. And they constructed—and held those dreams inside—a small twelve-foot by twelve-foot structure.

Those small cabins, of course, weren't constructed to last for centuries. They had a purpose for the moment. They provided a small level of protection from the elements for a season of time.

In contrast, let's consider the Roman Colosseum: The Colosseum or Coliseum, also known as the Flavian Amphitheatre, is an elliptical amphitheater in the center of the city of Rome, Italy. Built of concrete and stone, it was the largest amphitheater of the Roman Empire, and is considered one of the greatest works of Roman architecture and engineering. It is the largest amphitheater in the world.6

The Flavian Amphitheatre still stands after centuries. It was built to last. The arches in its construction are beautiful, but they also bear weight. Both sides of an arch press to the center. Any weight on top of an arch also presses the center together, giving it stability. How are so many arches in Rome still standing after thousands of years? Because the builders paid attention to their construction.

The problem with balancing working at home and raising kids is that we don't take time to construct something that will make it for the long haul. Instead of having Colosseum-thinking, we build one settler's cabin after another, doing our best to keep the elements at bay, and feeling very cramped in the process! We do this by just trying to get through the next month. By making excuses and telling ourselves, "I'll fix that tomorrow." We hammer boards together, made up of our schedule and tasks, hoping everything will work itself out in the end while inwardly knowing it won't.

As the Colosseum teaches us, good construction starts with the arch. Moms, you are the arch-builders in your family. (And I'm not talking about the Golden Arches!)

The famous arches built during the Roman Empire were created for ceremonial purposes to welcome returning heroes. Just as an arch bears weight, an arch also allows entrance. As the arch keeper in your home, you're the one in charge of what comes in—and goes out—of your schedule.

To prove he did his best work, a Roman architect would stand under his arch as the wooden supports were removed. Are you confident in how you are constructing your family and home life? Are you confident in what you are allowing in to your lives? Will your work stand? Will your family stand?

Mom, you are the architect of both your family and your career. In fact, the word "architect" comes from the word arch. In Greek, arkhitektōn is "director of works." Isn't that a perfect title for us as work-at-home moms?

No pressure, but the time and attention you give to the construction of your life will determine whether your family, goals, priorities, and work will stand the test of time. What are you building? Is it something that lasts?

Now don't get me wrong; there are seasons when we have to build temporary shelters to get us through. There may be a few months where everything piles up and you just do what you can to survive. But this shouldn't be the norm. Even with a full to-do list you can build your schedule to make sure the most important things get done. No wait . . . even more importantly, you can build a legacy that will stand the test of time. Remember it's up to you, the architect, to decide what you allow entrance to and what you don't.

How to Handle a Busy Schedule

Busy schedule? I understand.

Last spring, I had book deadlines April 1 and May 1 (with another project of devotions due April 15). We moved to a new house on April 1, and then I had a two-day trip the week of our move and a three-day trip the week after. And that was just the beginning of my to-do list!

I had a grandma to care for, a wonderful husband, and three kids at home. At that time, one child was in college, one in his last year of high school (whom I home-schooled), and a toddler! We also had another family living with us for a few weeks—five more people, including kids ages ten, seven, and five!

In addition to that were the daily responsibilities of being a writer: emails, phone calls, my weekly radio show, social media (Twitter, Facebook, and Pinterest, which I insist is work), and writing (of course!). To me social media is super fun and doesn't seem like work, but I did have some marketing stuff, too, because my novel about the Titanic, By the Light of the Silvery Moon, released March 1 and Beyond Hope's Valley released April 1.

How do I manage a schedule like that? The thing that helps me handle a schedule like that is to put everything into slots on my schedule on my computer. I use iCal, and I try to give everything a slot:

Morning quiet time

Time with my husband and kids

Homeschooling responsibilities

Running errands

Paying bills

Meetings

Phone interviews

Bible study

Blogs I need to write

Grocery shopping

Daily writing goals

Phone calls

Emails

Date nights

Small group

Church events

Housecleaning and laundry

Putting everything into my calendar gets it out of my brain. I don't have to think about it because I know I'll get to it. Each thing will get its turn, and each thing has to learn to be patient.

Then each morning, I prayerfully hold my schedule up to God and ask what He thinks of it. Sometimes I feel the need to scoot those to-dos off to another day and take my grandma to Walmart. Sometimes the list gets done faster than I thought and I have space for a nap. (And I take that nap, too, because all those other things I have to do are still in their spaces and are still waiting patiently for me!)

Sometimes my heart is moved in a different direction during morning devotions, or my mind is moved in a different direction by a book idea that won't stop hounding me. That's important, too. I've learned not to let my daily to-do list take control of my creativity. If I feel the Holy Spirit directing me to a new idea, I stop and listen to that. God knows my to-do list. I figure if He wants me to pause and redirect my creative energy, then He has the rest of the items on my to-do list figured out too!

God has also provided me with many wise advisers. I'll often adjust my daily calendar after talking with my husband. John's great about helping me pick out what's really important.

I also heed the advice of my agent, Janet Grant, who is great about telling me what idea can wait and what idea needs to be acted on now. I trust Janet, and her advice has been right ninety-nine percent of the time. (I personally can't remember the one percent when she wasn't right, but maybe there was a time?) Janet acts as a wise counselor to me, and having someone who can see the bigger picture when I tend to get focused on the daily, little stuff is important.

I also keep my heart tender to the needs of my kids. There are some days Alyssa needs more interaction and direction. There are days she's not content playing with play dough, sitting next to me as

I answer emails. There are times when she doesn't want a nap, and I've had to reschedule phone meetings I set up to be during her nap time. There are times she's sick and I've had to ask for a few extra days on a writing deadline. There are some days, nearer to book deadlines, when I find a babysitter so I can go to Panera to write.

(Note: The season I'm talking about was pre-two more kids. Bella [now six] and Casey [now three] joined our family this year, which makes scheduling even more fun... but you get the idea!)

My older kids need attention too. When my daughter wants to sit down and talk or my son asks if we can go to lunch—just the two of us—I make time. Sometimes I'm able to adjust my schedule that day, but if that's not possible, then I move other stuff aside and write them into my schedule as soon as possible.

For example, a few weeks ago Nathan asked if we could go to lunch, but I had a few phone meetings and some important errands that day. So we set a time for two days later. Knowing we were going to spend quality time together in a few days made us both happy.

As you know, life isn't always great about sticking to a schedule, but it's worth an effort to try to give everything a spot. Life happens, things change, and that's OK.

Give yourself grace for that. It's just easier for me to have everything written down where I can see it. Because iCal manages my to-dos, I do a better job of loving and caring for the people and tasks in the moment.

And maybe the most important element of scheduling is that I can see when my day is full. Yes, there are days I set in the schedule to write 2,000 words. Yes, there are days I plan to get caught up on laundry. But I know I can't do both in the same day. And I don't feel like a failure when both don't get done.

Being realistic helps me not to become stressed. I don't feel like a bad mom because I can't get it all done. Instead, I feel like a success because I made a plan. I also feel like a success when I push that plan aside for a time, knowing that the voice of the Holy Spirit knows a better way.

Pause and Reflect

iCal works for me, but consider what will work for you . How can you schedule your time and get those tasks off your mind? A sheet of paper and a pen will do . Start now! It doesn't matter what system you use, as much as the fact that you're doing it! And remember that when you put God first and your family second, all other things will fall into their proper place!

Tips from the Trenches

"Match your goals with the amount of time you have available to write. If you only have a couple of hours a week, setting a goal of writing a book in a year will only lead to disappointment. But maybe you can produce some articles or shorter pieces with that kind of time.

"Even small things, such as keeping a journal and reading books about writing, are steps in the right direction. As long as you are doing something, you are headed in the right direction.

"Join a critique group. It has built-in accountability in addition to getting feedback. When my kids were all babies, my only goal was to have two or three pages ready to share with my twice-a-month critique group.

"Find cheerleaders for your dreams. Sometimes it's your kids and your hubby, and sometimes it's your best friend. But everyone needs someone who believes in them."

—Novelist Sharon Dunn

Do What You Can, When You Can
{Another Great Tip}

It sounds obvious, but I'm going to go ahead and repeat it: Do what you can, when you can. What do I mean by this? Right now I'm sitting at my computer desk with stuff PILED on either side of me. I usually work on my notebook computer on the couch just because I don't like looking at these piles, but I can't because I spilled a drink on my notebook computer and it's no longer portable.

Right now two of my little ones are in their special therapy schools so only my three-year-old is at home. She's sitting in the computer chair behind me, playing a reading game. Of course she doesn't read, so I'm stopping about every ten seconds to help her. (I've probably stopped twenty times since I started writing the previous paragraph.)

As I sit down at the desk to work on email, the piles taunt me. And of course my daughter distracts me. As I try to answer important emails, a voice echoes in my head, "Just do what you can." It's then that I realized this motto is something I tell myself often.

When the house is a mess and I only have fifteen minutes to clean, I tell myself, "Just do what you can."

When I sit down to write and I only have fifteen minutes, I tell myself, "Just do what you can."

When I want to spend the whole day playing with my kids but I know the babysitter will be there in fifteen minutes, I tell myself, "Just play as you can—give what you can."

The amazing thing is those "do what you can" moments really add up. Or, as my friend (and novelist!) Traci DePree says, "Any progress is still progress." I love that!

I've discovered I can unload the dishwasher in just two minutes, and it only takes five minutes to sweep the floor. I can't write a whole scene or article in fifteen minutes, but I can jot down some notes, come up with a good hook, or write some compelling dialogue. And even though there are days when the babysitter is making lunch and taking my kids for a walk, my kids really do enjoy that fifteen minutes with me when I'm on the floor playing with them. They will remember those moments. And they really do enjoy time with our babysitter.

Yet too often we feel that if we don't have a full hour, it's not worth doing anything, giving anything.

We also allow guilt to plague us because we're not pouring ourselves out continually for our kids. It's just in the last thirty years that moms even entertained these thoughts. Through history children have been working alongside their parents. The woods, kitchen, and garden were their playgrounds. They entertained themselves while their parents worked. And in turn they learned how to work themselves.

Yes, I still feel guilty at times when I'm not constantly playing with my little kids, but I've learned that when little kids learn to entertain themselves through reading and play, they become big kids who entertain themselves. They also grow into adults who "entertain" themselves through reading and discovering new interests.

My kids learn how to use their imaginations. Our culture is so used to keeping kids moving. We're afraid they'll get bored, but given the right tools and direction boredom can lead to the growth of imagination. Play leads to creativity, and creativity leads to successful teens and adults . . . and to think I felt guilty for fostering that!

"Just do what you can" is being creative in the moment with the time I've been given, and it's amazing how much really gets done in the end!

Tips from the Trenches

"For our women's Bible study we are using the book The Beautiful Wife by Sandy Ralya. LOVE this book! In it she too talks about balancing our passions and our priorities. Here is one quote from Sandy: 'The Lord will never ask you to sacrifice your priorities (your relationship with Him, your husband and your children) to follow your passion.' She emphasizes you need to be aware of what season of life you're in, realizing there are times when you will only be able to spend a few minutes each day on your passion because you have active, young children or you are working outside your home. But that's OK. There will be other seasons when you have more discretionary time. Kids grow up and leave home; you only have a few years to invest in their lives. You will be so glad you did!"

—Novelist Carrie Turansky

Chapter Seven

Successful {Not Stressful} Family Living

A dozen or so years ago, I spoke to a friend on the phone, spilling my concerns about my packed calendar. I had kids to homeschool, books to write, mentor responsibilities—not to mention the daily stuff that comes up.

"At least a few times a week my grandma needs a ride into town for errands," I explained. "And then there are the kids. There is always last-minute stuff: figuring out the right homeschooling homework, play dates with friends, and church activities."

My friend listened, and then answered with a sigh. "It sounds like you've set yourself up for failure. Without a plan, you leave everyone vying for a piece of you. What if your grandma had a set day when you'd take her to town? Do you think she could get everything squeezed into one afternoon?"

"What if your kids knew which day was shopping day?" she continued. "Could they come up with a list of their needs? Or better yet, could they help with the shopping? And what about your freelance work— could you schedule days for certain things?"

Her idea was brilliant, and I wondered why I hadn't thought of it sooner myself. As soon as I got off the phone, I started working on a plan. I started with my grandma first, setting up a weekly date for breakfast and errands. That worked so well, I began scheduling grocery shopping and my kids' weekly chores, too.

I also decided to take a look at what I was doing and why. Were these things I truly wanted to do, or was I simply trying to meet someone else's expectations? Oh yes, I also decided to enlist help with the new system.

Teamwork Works!

In the past, I'd assumed all household and family responsibilities rested on my shoulders (another way I set myself up for failure). I've since discovered that

John likes working on our schedule with me. In fact, most guys are eager to step up to the plate when given the chance.

As I shared my plans and tasks with John, he had great insight when it came to kids, chores, and activities. "Spending time with the family" sometimes means cleaning out the garage or raking fall leaves. But as we remind our kids, "Many hands make light work." Our system also creates space for playtime!

Here are three more ideas we've embraced:

1. Focus on Family

It's been said that what you spend your days doing will determine what you spend your lifetime doing. There's a lot of truth in that. Five years from now, I don't want to look back and regret not spending enough time with my friends, my children, or my spouse.

I'm often guilty of focusing on the wrong things. I worry what my neighbor thinks about the weeds growing in my flowerbed while completely ignoring the fact that I haven't had a heart-to-heart conversation with John in weeks. I spend an hour decorating cookies for the church bake sale, and then tell my family to fend for themselves when it comes to dinner.

"Our choice reveals what we love the most, what we fear, what is of ultimate value to us, and what we think we need in life—in other words, our choices expose the dominant desires of our heart," writes Leslie Vernick, author of How to Act Right When Your Spouse Acts Wrong.7

To put it another way: Jesus said, "For what will it profit a man if he gains the whole world, and loses his own soul?" Mark 8:36 (NKJV).

Likewise, what does it profit my family if I'm known for the best school lunches, volunteer at the local rest home, or keep in shape by committing to daily exercise but I don't spend time with the people I've committed to love forever? Focusing on my family looks different on different days. It means smiles around the table. Playing with pots and pans in the living room and not yelling (too loudly) when the kids dump all of the clothes from their drawers on to the floor. It's knowing I don't gain anything if I'm not joyful in my home.

2. Step Out of the Safety Zone

My nature is to live a safe and simple life. To hang out with people who are just like me. To keep my house clean. To keep my schedule organized. Only to do things I feel are in my comfort zone. To put a safety net around me, my work, and my kids. I want to have complete control over what I do and do it well.

The fact is, as a work-at-home mom you will not be able to work, care for kids, and keep a clean house all at the same time. (You should see my living room right now— TOYS everywhere!)

Yet I'm learning not to stress in the mess. I'm learning to trust that people will love me even if my house isn't perfect. Will life really fall apart if I leave the dishes in the sink overnight? (It won't; I've tried it!) I don't want to pass up making a memory in order to clean a kitchen that will be dirty again tomorrow.

Don't get me wrong; I don't like things this way. I just choose to focus on more important things. I still worry: What if my friend stops by and sees the mess? What will my neighbor think if the floor hasn't been swept? In fact my friends have stopped by when the house is a mess, and you know what? They understand. I work at home and have three preschoolers running around for goodness' sake! "Pressures come from two directions: what other people expect of us and what we expect of ourselves," say Dennis and Barbara Rainey, authors of Staying Close: Stopping the Natural Drift toward Isolation in Marriage. "It is so easy to let yourself be driven by the agendas of other people. Externally, their voices form a deafening chorus, incessantly telling us what we ought to do."8

For me, not giving in to the agendas of other people means not worrying so much about making everything perfect in case someone comes over. It means stepping out of the safety zone. So what if everything isn't perfect— especially if perfection means a cranky, frantic family?

Instead, I'm paying attention to the messages I send my family. I don't ever want to give them the impression that the house—or those cupcakes—are more important than they are. Every day around here is an important one, so if my house isn't beautiful I'll try to make my heart more beautiful to compensate!

3. Remember that Rigid People are Brittle and Break Easily

Have you ever been tense, rigid, and feel as if you're going to break if one more responsibility is placed upon your shoulders? Yeah, me too. The problem starts with our unrealistic expectations. I become rigid, thinking I should be able to do more than is humanly possible. And then I beat myself up for it when I can't reach my goals!

I'm trying to be more flexible. I'm learning to give myself grace just as God gives me grace. Why do I insist on being harder on myself than God is? It only brings fretting. A lot of us bring down our family's morale by being too unrealistic about the little things that don't matter. If I want my husband

and kids to help me succeed, I need to affirm their efforts, even if those efforts are not what I consider perfect. How discouraging it is when your child attempts to help only to be told they didn't do it well enough? If I'm causing them to stress over my unrealistic expectations, then I'm creating rigid little people who are brittle and break easily too! So instead of being rigid about getting everything done perfectly, I choose to be intentional about who I am in ALL parts of my life: my work, my relationships with my family, and my attitude. What are my choices doing to me? Are they helping me become the person God wants me to be?

Intentionality can be a lifestyle. And I'm not talking about over-scheduling my life—filling in little calendar squares—to the point that I need to carry a day planner 24/7. Instead, each week I look over my to-do list and see what matters in light of being intentional. The scheduling technique I mentioned in the last chapter works great!

In the war between rigidity and intentionality I replay this phrase in my mind: "Set yourself up for success, not failure." This helps me choose the right approach when I make a plan to meet my family's needs . . . and when I seek their help in meeting some of my needs in return.

But most of my true spiritual success comes when things don't turn out as planned, when the house is a mess, the kids act up, I miss a deadline, but I'm able to keep a godly attitude. It's then I realize this journey isn't about one day, one moment. This journey is about love, faithfulness, obedience, and service for the long haul.

Pause and Reflect

How can you be more intentional about your daily living?

How can you be more intentional about your attitude and heart?

How can my family be part of the team—how can we work together for the benefit of our home?

How can I use my expectations to benefit me, not to hurt me?

Tips from the Trenches

Leslie Vernick says, "Our choice reveals what we love the most, what we fear, what is of ultimate value to us, and what we think we need in life—in other words, our choices expose the dominant desires of our heart."

"'It's hard to know, isn't it, whether the things we face are just because the world is full of sin and sinful people, or if God is working out a plan,' Grandma continued. 'I happen to think it's both. There's sin, but through it all, He takes the mess we make and paints a masterpiece. In fact, I'm quite certain that before God can ever bless a woman—and use her to impact many—He uses the hammer, the file, and the furnace to do a holy work.'"

—Tricia Goyer and Ocieanna Fleiss,
Love Finds You in Glacier Bay, Alaska

For the Writer Moms

Below is a quote from author, Dr. Saundra Dalton-Smith:

As a full-time physician, mom of two boys, and writer, I've had to learn a few tricks to staying motivated in all three roles. Here are a few of my tips on mothering and writing:

1. Let your kids help you tell the story. When I'm not feeling creative due to stress and feeling overwhelmed, my boys are always full of imagination and creative release! Next time you can't think about another topic to write about, ask your kids to tell you about their day. Listen as they explain what excited them and why they found it exciting. Before you know it, something they say will spark a creative release and renewed insight.

2. Post-It. Put Post-It note pads in the places you typically get creative thoughts (nightstand drawer, ash tray in car, purse, office desk drawer). This way when a phrase from a song on the radio grabs your heart you can jot it down or when a divine download gives you the outline for your next book you will be ready to capture it. I find this works better than trying to

type it on my Smartphone, since I don't usually take my phone to bed with me!

3. Live to tell your story. Some of the best writing is born out of struggle and difficulty. If you are going through something, chances are so is another mom, even if it seems like a problem that is uncommon. Live your story out loud, in the open, without apology or pretense, and share your story with everyone who stops by your blog or within the pages of the books you write. No one is an expert about everything, but everyone is an expert about their story.

Being Creative Benefits Everyone

When I set off on this path to be a work-at-home mom, I had a few things on my mind and heart. I didn't want someone else watching my kids all day so I could work, yet I couldn't imagine not pouring my time into something meaningful and creative. I wanted to be influential in numerous arenas, in my home and out of it. And the truth is I'm a happy mom when I allow myself to be creative!

But I'd be lying to say I had pure motives when I set out to write books. I didn't become a writer for the pure joy of writing or even for the self-sacrificing reason of reaching the world for Christ. Choosing that for my work-at-home field was about more than just expressing my creativity. I was also trying to prove myself. I wanted to prove that a former teenage mom could amount to something. I wanted to get a book published. I wanted worth.

Yet what I discovered was so much more than that. Mostly I learned a lot about myself, and I found healing through my work.

At first, I learned how closed-off I was becoming from getting rejection after rejection. The writing rejections brought back old hurts I realized I hadn't dealt with, feelings of insecurity, being judged. After all, if a publisher didn't like my book they must not like me.

God soon showed me that my worth doesn't come from whether I sold a book or not, and it wasn't diminished by the bad choices I'd made in my youth—I was loved by Him. That was enough. Then when I opened my heart, I sold my first book. Why? Because what I was writing resonated with hurting people.

That discovery led to an important truth: Working at home will break you at times, but it's only when we're broken that God can take those pieces and bring healing and transformation. He could create a beautiful mosaic from my mess.

God placed creativity within me, but it wasn't just something I could turn on and off like a spigot. I needed to depend on God to help my creative juices flow.

I discovered that God wanted to pour out messages of hope through me, but to do it I had to depend on Him completely, especially as we added children to our family and life got busier. I also discovered I was the key audience for my own messages. I could only write worthwhile content when I walked with God, listened to God, and knew God intimately. If anything I wrote was going to be of use to another person, it was because God spoke to me about it first.

My work-at-home journey moved from me trying to prove myself to allowing God to prove what He could do through a weak vessel like me. And it turned out that it was A LOT! So in the end, He gets the glory, which is what it should have been all about in the first place.

Friend, if God is leading you to work at home, He can help you there. You can make money and be a good parent, too. You can express your creativity in amazing ways, but don't limit this journey to those things. Dedicate this journey in such a way that you turn to God and depend on Him more and more. Don't feel you have to know everything and do everything. Instead, keep your ear open to the whisper of the Holy Spirit who truly understands balance in a way we never will.

As a work-at-home writer, my goal is to live what I write and to love the Lord and my family as much I say I do in print. I know Jesus Christ can make a difference in my life today, and when I allow Him to do that it transforms my work and my family.

Jesus Christ can make a difference in your life today as you embrace His truth and strive to live it out. God isn't simply a figure in history, but He can forever change your history—your family's history—if you let Him!

The divine life is meant to work itself out in daily living. When you come to God as a work-at-home mom and turn over your work, your family, and your creativity to Him, that's exactly what can happen. As for me, when I set off on this path to be a work-at-home mom I had a few things on my mind and heart, but God has done even more than I ever imagined. Now, I'm able to stay at home. I'm able to be with my kids for much of the day, and I'm doing meaningful and creative work! I'm influential, not because I had anything of worth to share. Instead, I'm influential because I allow God to be the greatest influence in my life. I allow Him into my heart, to do His holy work, and then I allow Him to pour His messages out for His glory.

Often the "Work" Starts Within

There are many jobs you can do without really giving much thought to it. But if your work-at-home job includes writing, you might have to come to terms with the idea that what's on the inside is what comes out. There is no faking it—at least not for long. You reap what you sow when it comes to your character. You reap it in your attitude. You reap it in your relationships. And you even reap it in your work.

Character is the foundation of your role as a dedicated worker and a mom. Do you need to tear down a wall between you and God? He's eager to do that. Are you hiding something? God wants you to work and parent in freedom, not in bondage to past mistakes or sins.

You can follow every tip offered, but only your connection with the Holy Spirit, listening to Him and letting Him work in your heart, will transform everything. You may wonder what this has to do with balance.

Hiding what hurts is hard work. It takes time. It binds you. It takes you way off-balance.

I'd tried to write for a few years while hiding the fact I'd had an abortion. My writing was dead, flat. My emotions toward my kids were seized up. When I found freedom from my sin through God's healing and when I started helping others find the same healing, my spirit was open to God. The walls came down. The words began to flow, and my work succeeded. Becoming successful is as much about the changes the work does in you as it is about transformation in others through your work.

Do you want to write? Be as real with yourself as possible. Is there something you've been hiding? Take it before God. It's only then the walls come down. And when the walls come down, the messages march out one by one by one.

Tips from the Trenches

"If the entire day is a writing day but the little one is at home, I select a few fifteen-minute intervals spread throughout the day that are simply for her. After writing a while, I head into her room and sit down with her. I set the timer, and I let her know that it is

Lacey time and we can play whatever game she wants for those fifteen minutes because they are hers. She knows the time is coming, and she loves it when it's there. It helps her when I return to work for another long stretch."

Chapter Eight

I Can't Tell You How Many Times a Week I'm Asked, "How Do You Do It All?"

I can't tell you how many times a week I'm asked, "How do you do it all?" My answer is, "I don't." But from the smiles, nods, and looks I get, I don't think people believe me.

Honestly, people, I can't do it all. Or as they say in the south, "Bless your heart," for thinking I do. Some things I haven't done lately:

- Put away my laundry
- Dealt with the pile of mail in the kitchen
- Painted my fingernails (haven't done this in a year)
- Returned some calls (yeah, need to do that)
- Cleaned my bedroom/office
- Finished some ebooks that are mostly done (Ha! I can take this ebook off that list!)

- Shopped . At all . OK, I get groceries, but that's about it
- Had weekly date nights with my husband as I know I should
- Watched television—even the shows I really, really like
- Called to talk to long-distance family

I also had to say no to some awesome church events I wanted to attend but just couldn't squeeze in.
These are all things I have on my immediate to-do list. Well, not the shopping, although I know the girls in my house would really like a day out with me.

Work-wise, I don't do it all, either. Right now I have a book I really need to finish and another book I need to edit, and two more that need my attention ASAP but are patiently waiting their turn.

There are blogs I need to write and marketing tasks I need to get busy on. In fact I'm having a book-signing in a few weeks, and I better spread the word or I'll be sitting in the store alone that day. Sigh.

I've had to say no to two writing projects recently—things I really wanted to do but just don't have the time for. Yes, my done list is impressive at times, but the battle rages within when I know there is so much more want to than I have time or energy for. But I'm learning to be OK with not being able to do everything. It's how God made me. Instead I have a list in my mind of things that are most important, and I focus on these:

- Time with God each day
- Some type of exercise
- Morning prayer and conversation with my husband
- Story time, snuggle time, bath time, and playtime with my preschoolers
- Having at least one "focus-on-their-eyes" conversation with each person in our home (there are seven people currently, so this alone takes a while)
- My most important emails and most important deadlines

• "Future work," like ideas and proposals to keep the ball rolling

• Dinner together as a family and hang-out time, too, every day

So, do you believe me now that I don't do it all? I hope you'll be encouraged. There's always a balance with what we can do, need to do, and have to do. The only way I can stay somewhat balanced is to focus on Jesus, keep my eyes on Him, and have Him point out what's most important. Sometimes that's getting my house in order so I can offer hospitality, and sometimes it's jotting off an idea and sending it to my agent, even though twenty other emails seem more important at the time.

Jesus knows what is important from an eternal standpoint—I need to trust that. As I turn my mind to Him during the day, I have peace as we walk side-by-side—even if it means ignoring that pile of mail or stepping over the laundry until tomorrow . . . which brings me to something important we need to talk about: how to know God's voice.

Yes, you can learn to listen to God's voice in your work

Think about the men who God called out in service for Him. Peter and James were called when they were fishing. Elijah was plowing. Moses was tending sheep. Many times Jesus taps you on the shoulder when you're busy doing other stuff. I'd say eighty percent of my really good work ideas come when I'm sweeping, doing laundry, or bathing kids. The key is to write them down so you don't forget them!

In the book, Mr. Jones, Meet The Master, Peter Marshall prays the following prayer:

"O God our Father, history and experience have given us so many evidences of Thy guidance to nations and to individuals that we should not doubt Thy power of Thy willingness to direct us. Give us the faith to believe that when God wants us to do or not to do any particular thing, God finds a way of letting us know.

"May we not make it more difficult for Thee to guide us, but be willing to be led of Thee, that Thy will may be done in us and through us for the good of America and all mankind. This we ask in Jesus' name. AMEN."9

I was reminded of this prayer as I watched End of the Spear this afternoon. Many years ago, five missionaries ventured out to share the Good News of Jesus with a vicious tribe of people. Their plane was to fly into a remote area where tribesmen had not heard of the love of Jesus and to build relationships with the tribesmen. Yet when their plane landed on the remote river setting, things went terribly wrong. The tribesmen turned against them, slaughtering them all. The missionaries never had a chance to tell of Jesus' love and died on the river rocks. Yet later others followed, sharing the Good News and the hearts of the natives changed. Not only that, the stories of the men went around the world, reach many, many lives. It was also made into a major motion picture.

These missionaries had no idea that years after those tribesmen slaughtered them on the beach millions of people would know their story, and the story of how their widows then brought the Gospel to the tribe, transforming them for Christ, and moviegoers would be hearing their message over and over again. It was more than they could have ever imagined. Their work—though not what they expected—was not in vain. They were called by God, and they followed. God let them know their part of His plan, and then He used their sacrifice to impact His kingdom.

Personally, I've come to trust that Marshall's words are true, ". . . when God wants us to do or not to do any particular thing, God finds a way of letting us know." I trust that because it has been true in my life.

There are many instances when God places something on my heart, and I may never know why. Then there are other times when I listen, obey, and am allowed a glimpse of what God is up to.

A number of summers ago, that very thing happened to me. After conversations with other moms my mind started thinking about how the parenting of my generation was different from the one before me. Then I came across some amazing statistics, such as the fact that the divorce rate raised 300% during the growing-up years of Gen Xers, meaning that they not only faced the divorce of their parents, but often step-parents too. Many of these couples were swinging the opposite direction, trying to raise their children differently than they'd been raised. Reading this, God placed it on my heart to write a book for Generation X parents. I had another book under deadline, a conference to prepare for, schoolwork to organize for my kids, but I couldn't shake the thought. Putting together a proposal for this book was something I felt that I had to do right then.

Within a month, I had a proposal submitted to my agent. Within another month we received word that a few publishers were interested. And by November 15, we heard that Multnomah Publishers, one of the best publishers in the business, was offering a contract! The finished product hit the shelves September 15, 2006 . . . one year from the time God placed the idea on my heart.

I have no clue how many people the message of that book touched, and that's OK. I can't do much concerning results, but I can be obedient in following God in the areas He calls me to.

Many years ago, five missionaries walked in obedience, and it cost them their lives. But, oh, how many hearts have been touched by their story. This year, God is leading me down numerous paths of publication . . . yet I'm leaving the results to Him.

Now, what about you? Are you willing to pray the same prayer? Are you willing to trust God with your work? Are you willing to listen to His still, small voice?

Can you pray this: "Lord, give me the faith to believe that when You want me to do or not to do any particular thing, You will find a way of letting me know."

I guarantee if you expect and believe, He won't let you down.

God Speaks to Bring Change

Every day we have access to our God who longs to speak to us. Our God who is able to strengthen us. Who can give us wisdom. Who longs to guide our steps.

Jesus has a perfect plan for our lives. We may wonder where to commit ourselves and our time, but Jesus doesn't have to wonder. He knows what investment of our time, effort, and energy will bring the biggest yield. He knows the people He wants us to connect with. He knows how a simple game, a cuddly moment, or a heart-to-heart discussion with one of our kids can make a forever memory. It might even be a spiritual turning point in the lives of one of our kids.

Working from home while raising kids for the last twenty years has shown me that God knows what He's doing. It's fueled my faith. It has tuned my listening skills and softened my heart to God's agenda and not my own. I am changed as I put myself in God's hands—as I listen to His voice.

This isn't my gig. It's not my life to figure out. I dedicated my life to God; it's His! I have to keep reminding myself of that.

When I first prayed a prayer of surrender—giving my life to God—I said, "If you can do anything with my life, please do."

I gave Jesus my everything, and there have been many, many times when I've tried to take control back, but when I leave it in Jesus' hands He does exceedingly more than I could ask or imagine. How foolish for me to think that I, with my limited knowledge and no concept of what's coming in the future, could do a better job at figuring out where to spend my time and energy, compared to a holy God. God is wisdom and truth, and He knows not only the past but the future.

There are times when we face suffering as a Christian. Bad things happen to the godly and ungodly. We live in a fallen world full of sin. There is sickness and pain. There is loss and regret, but God brings situations into your life to mold you, to change you to be more like Christ. When you feel uncertain about what direction to take, the Holy Spirit wants to be your counselor. The Holy Spirit is good about pointing you in the right way; you just have to seek Him and be willing to listen. The way might not always be easy, but God has a good plan for you—one that will impact His kingdom if you let it.

When I look to Jesus, He will not leave me stranded or disappointed. Even the roads I walk that leave me feeling weak or uncertain have a purpose in His agenda. Even the wilderness places have a chapter in the God-story that I'm allowing Him to write with my life. For me it's a story I never expected, but one I would never want to change.

Tips from the Trenches

This is a text message thread from me to my husband John. (I thought you'd enjoy the typos, too):

Me> Alyssa has been crying to two hours. I've been trying to very her to nap. On the couch, in our bed. Now she's in her beef.
Me> Now she's in her bed.

Me> I haven't written a world all day. I'm exhausted, overwhelmed and I need your help.

John> I love you and am honored to help. I will take her out of your hair when I get home.

Me> I love you.

Have you ever had a day like that?! I'm so thankful for my dear husband who cared for our little one after he got home from a long day at work and after I fed him chicken nuggets for dinner!

Also, does that sound like someone who is able to do it all?

I told you, I don't! But God is good all the time.

How to Make Today Truly Miserable (Unofficial Un-recommended List):

• Open your eyes in the morning and think of all you didn't get done yesterday .

• Assume your husband has a huge list of things for you to do when he asks, "So, do you have any plans today?" (as if you didn't have a huge to-do list every day) .

• Push aside your Bible reading and jump into sorting that stinky pile of laundry .

• Remember what it used to feel like to wear your skinny, skinny jeans .

• Compare your kids to your neighbors' star athletes and whiz kids .

• Compare your house/office/yard to the awesome pictures continually reposted on Pinterest .

• Walk the mall and point out all the things you wish you had money to buy .

Or . . .

How to Make Today Truly Amazing (Unofficial Recommended List):

• Thank God for everything your new day holds .

• Give your husband a hug and ask if he has something special in mind for the day . If he doesn't, tell him you do   and do something spontaneous .

• Take time to read your Bible and ask the Creator of the universe to guide your day .

• Appreciate your health and pray asking God to help you in all areas where you are weak . Or if you have a chronic illness thank Him for walking you through it .

• Hug your kids and tell them what you appreciate the most about who God made them to be .

• Relax in your favorite part of your house for ten minutes and thank God for what He's provided .

• Go through your closet and pull out clothes you haven't worn in a while—then take them to Goodwill .

Which list would you rather follow?

Tips from the Trenches:

A few words from Janet McHenry, a seasoned mom of four adult children and nana to eight grandchildren, author of Prayer Changes Teens: How to Parent From Your Knees, as well as a full-time high school teacher:

1. Choose God first
2. Choose family second
3. The rest will fall into place

How I've had to choose family over my full-time teaching job:

1. Taking two weeks off from school to help my daughter Rebekah with her first baby, Josiah (who ended up being in NICU for a week—born not breathing, brought back to life)
2. Missing some afternoon hours at work to transport my daughter Bethany to basketball games
3. Taking a couple days off to take son Joshua to college for the first time. Never, ever "send" your kid to college; always take your child. Those goodbye moments are too precious to miss.

My husband, Craig, and I also thought it was important that our children also learn to play at least one sport and one musical instrument. They are now athletically fit and active—and all musical in their own ways. Together they played baseball, basketball, and soccer, and ran track. Among them they play these instruments: piano, guitar, flute, and the bagpipes. Justin mostly plays the barbecue, but that's another story!

Ponder This:

"When you want what God wants for the reasons God wants it you're unstoppable . . . for the glory of God."
—Steven Furtick, pastor at Elevation Church

Chapter Nine

Being a Mom AND Following Your God-Given Dreams...I Give You Permission

My face glows when I talk about my latest writing projects. I've always loved reading and creating stories. During my childhood summers when my friends were at the lake, I was in the library. Looking back, I can see early hints of the dreams God placed deep inside. But the contentment I feel when I use my talents and follow my dreams is something many people wish they had.

One afternoon I saw a wistful look in my friend Stacey's eyes as she squeezed a few minutes out of her busy day to talk with me over a glass of tea.

"I wish I had something of my own," this mother of three small boys confessed. "Some type of special purpose I knew was from God."

As Stacey spoke, I squinted and looked closely at her. Yes, under that baby-food stained T-shirt she did have something of her own. Stacey's heart was filled with dreams lying dormant, waiting to be awakened.

Sometimes we, like Stacey, don't know our dreams are there. We feel incomplete but don't understand why. Other times the fulfillment of our dreams is stunted by outside factors—not enough time, not enough energy, and too many duties filling up our days (especially with kids).

But most of all we just need permission. Permission to slow down. Permission to discover our deepest purpose. And permission to follow God-breathed dreams even when we still have kids at home. I've written books and articles while raising kids, and although at times I felt guilty for not being able to watch a movie with them or for feeding them pizza for dinner— again—I'm a good mom. We sit around the table at dinner. I take time with each child each day. We serve together; we laugh together. Once I started following God's dreams for me, I've also been an example to my children of what following God-dreams looks like.

So what are God's dreams for you? Here is a good question to ask: "If I could be doing anything for God's kingdom what would it be?"

A second question is as equally important: "What is God asking me to do now in this season I'm in?" Once we have given ourselves permission to dream, the next step is granting ourselves freedom to follow through. This acronym can help F-R-E-E-D-O-M:

Find time to spend with God. Ask Him to show you how to make the most of your potential.

Research the area you want to pursue. For example, if
you desire to develop your talent in art, discover what's available at your local community college, or call art supply shops for information about classes.

Expect to make adjustments to your schedule. Focusing on God's calling for your life will not be easy. Make a list of your daily responsibilities and decide which are important and which are simply time-consumers. Also, decide which duties follow the path God has called you to. Sometimes even good things are not the right things. You might teach Sunday school and run a food ministry, but perhaps that leaves you unable to follow a deeper desire to work with the elderly.

Enjoy the process of striving toward your dream. Oswald Chambers says in My Utmost for His Highest, "We have the idea that God is leading us toward a particular end or a desired goal, but He is not. What we see as only the process of reaching a particular end, God sees as the goal itself."

Develop relationships with others who share the same talents and goals. Be available for encouragement and prayer.

Openly communicate your dreams to your family, and ask them to share theirs. Brainstorm ways to help one another reach God's best. While you are working toward the dreams God has given you, help your husband and children to follow their God-given dreams.

Make daily appointments with God to ensure you are on the right track. Many of us have the tendency to take our dreams and run in a direction God never intended. God will never ask you to follow Him if it means turning your back on your family. Getting excited about your calling is easy, but remember that as you take care of those in your home, God will be watering your dreams and breathing life into them in ways you can't see.

"How often do you get caught up in the daily agenda, making lists of what to do, losing sight of your own and others' deepest needs? We attend to the dishes, laundry, carpool, phone calls, and faxes, but not to each other."
—Becky Bailey, Ph.D., I Love Your Rituals10

God-Given Dreams Take Care

In order to follow our dreams it's important to care for ourselves—and our creativity—in numerous ways. Here are a few:

1. Find One Person Who Understands
Most people will not truly be able to understand what it means to balance working at home and being a

parent. My husband lives with me, yet he doesn't understand the writing part (not all of it). My agent and assistant keep tabs on all my work, but even they don't understand the kid part. It's OK if not everyone understands. But, if possible, find a few people—even if they live far away—who can "talk the talk" with you.

My friend Cindy—whom I started this writing journey with—is also a professional writer, mom of older kids, and mom of little ones too. When we chat, we laugh about how crazy our lives are. We share with humor and grace the ups and downs of the balancing act!

2. Care for Yourself

When I'm asked to fill out author questionnaires I'm often asked about my hobbies. Hello? I have six kids, I write numerous books a year, and I run our teen mom support group. Who has time for hobbies?

While I don't take time to enroll in an art class, crochet a baby blanket, or work in my garden, I do have some me time. I enjoy riding on my exercise bike and reading. (I can't just sit still and read very often; it feels too indulgent!) I enjoy morning quiet time before the kids are awake. I enjoy cooking and browsing through bookstores, libraries, and antique shops.

Even though it's hard to find the time, I make appointments for haircuts, Bible studies, and an occasional coffee with friends. We need to take care of ourselves to the best of our ability—not just for us but for our families too.

When we feel rested and healthy our whole family benefits. If we aren't physically, spiritually, and emotionally healthy, what good will we be to anyone? It's another place we need balance. We don't want to spend too much time indulging ourselves, but we also need to make sure we care for ourselves. And just as we need to care for our body, soul, and spirit, we need to care for our creative lives too.

3. Be Inspired

Being creative is hard when there are people and paperwork and piles to manage. When I look around my house and see the walls that need to be painted and the cupboards that should be organized. When my inbox is cluttered with notes I need to answer about work stuff and volunteer stuff. When output is more than input. It's hard not to be overwhelmed much less creative.

What can you do when you need an extra spark of inspiration? Here are a few things I do.

- Call a friend with a good sense of humor .
- Sit outside . Breathe in fresh air . Listen to birdsongs . Watch busy ants .
- Open a book of poetry . Absorb the symbolism and fresh word combinations .
- Open a cookbook and find a recipe of something you'd like to make but never tried before . (Then go shopping .)
- Go to YouTube.com and watch old dance numbers .
- Visit Etsy.com . Enjoy the fresh colors, textures, and ideas .

• Play at Visuwords.com . Follow word trails and see where they lead you .

• Have a visual feast at iStockPhoto.com

• Pray and thank God for His creativity . Thank Him for your favorite places, people, tastes, and the beauty of nature .

• Read your favorite Bible verses in a version you normally don't read . Here is my favorite Bible verse in The Message (Zephaniah 3:17): "Don't be afraid . Dear Zion, don't despair . Your God is present among you, a strong Warrior there to save you . Happy to have you back, he'll calm you with his love and delight you with his songs ."

• Write a greeting card verse and send it to a special person .

4. Be Open to Change

I'm a person who thrives on routine. Every morning I make coffee, slip away for a few minutes of Bible study, shower, and eat the same breakfast—a protein shake. For date nights with my husband, John, I want to eat at the same restaurants. During the day, I visit the same websites, read the same blogs, and interact with the same friends. And in the funny way life works, my schedule seems to be one of constant change. I homeschool my kids, which means new subjects and assignments daily. Under various deadlines, I write books about ever-changing topics. I can't count on summer breaks, Saturday lazy days, or even sleep.

As if that wasn't enough, I've been through BIG changes. Like when I felt drawn to launch a crisis pregnancy center. After that, my heart was tugged to lead Teen MOPS—and deal with teenage moms who are in a crisis of change in their lives! And for four years, our family traveled to the Czech Republic where we taught English at a family camp. New culture, new food, new language, oh my! And then we added three kids through adoption. And if that wasn't enough God asked us to move 2,000 miles from the northwest to the south! In fact, the only thing that hasn't changed is that all my children still need me. (I have a feeling that will never change.)

Without change always happening, I'd be happy within my four walls—left picking lint off the floor and stressing over fingerprints on the windows, which I've been known to do. You might think I'd be feeling a little perturbed with God by now. I mean, He made me one way and pushed me to act another by stirring my heart and my compassion. But instead of being mad, I'm thankful.

I'm happy I'm pushed out of my comfort zone at times because it's there I find God. I discover He not only equips me and meets my needs, but He's present through every change—comforting, guiding, and encouraging me with His joy and peace.

Is change happening in your life right now? Yup, that's to be expected. Are you eager yet scared, hopeful yet anxious? That's understandable. Just remember that even though you'd rather everything stayed the same, God is waiting for you—often just beyond your comfort zone. He's there with open arms, prepared to walk with you every step of the ever-changing way.

And that's something that will never change.

Tips from the Trenches

"I was a single mom of pre-teen daughters and had a full- time, eight-to-five job when I started writing my first book. By the time I'd sold my first and second novels, I developed a schedule and kept to it most of the time. Monday through Thursday, I came home from work and fixed and ate dinner with my daughters. By 7:00, I was at my computer, and I wrote until 9:00. I also wrote on Saturday mornings when the girls slept in. Friday evenings, Saturday afternoons, and all-day Sundays were family time. Also, I had an 'open door' policy. The girls could interrupt me anytime they needed to. They were my top priority, not the writing. I wrote and had nine books published during a nine-year period before I quit my job to write full-time. By then, both of my daughters were grown and on their own. My main tip is this: Write something every day. If you write just one page per day, you will have a 365-page novel at the end of a year."

—Best-selling novelist Robin Lee Hatcher

"Everything can be taken from a man but one thing: the last of the human freedoms—to choose one's attitude in any given set of circumstances, to choose one's own way."

—Viktor E. Frankl, Man's Search for Meaning

Chapter Ten
The Freedom of Knowing Yourself

I remember a time in my life (OK, more than one) when I became so busy serving God—working for him—that I didn't have time for Him.

"But Martha was distracted with much serving. And she went up to him and said, 'Lord, do you not care that my sister has left me to serve alone? Tell her then to help me,'" Luke 10:40 (ESV).

You may think, like Martha, that if you don't do the work, it's not going to get done—and that's a good possibility. And yet one question I ask myself is, "What really needs to be done today?"

One problem with working at home, caring for children at home, and serving God from home is that you never leave your work! I've been jealous at times of people who leave their day job, turn off their computer, drive home, and are done. I don't know about you, but my work calls to me and taunts me.

My work is almost always on my thoughts. The laundry pile is heavy on my thoughts too, especially when I have to step over it to walk down the hall.

I've gotten good about asking myself what REALLY needs to get done today. It's then I make plans to pick one or two things for my to-do list. This is the real to-do list that I listen to. I also consciously put everything else on my "to-don't-do" list. When I walk by the laundry pile I tell it, "I'm not going to worry about you today." I do the same with the 300 emails in my inbox and the other work projects that haven't made their way to the to-do list. I've become a master at ignoring what I haven't picked as my tasks for the day.

The truth is that we are human and we can only do so much in a day.

The truth is that spending time with our kids, cooking a family dinner, and spending time with God—reading our Bible and praying—are important things.

The truth is the important things will get pushed to the side if we let other projects press into that space.

Making a to-do list is like erecting a fence around the tasks we deem most important for the day. It protects the important tasks and gives us a bit of wiggle room around our other tasks.

This one is hard for me. Currently, I live fifteen minutes from our church, which is in inner-city Little Rock. There are very real needs right down the street. In my outreach to teen moms, I know young women with children who don't have enough food in the cupboards. There are teens who are going to miss school that day because their baby is sick and can't go to daycare. There are young women who really need a listening ear. Yet God keeps reminding me that while I can do some things, I can't do everything. I can do the tasks He asks and recruit others to help . . . but then I must trust Him for the rest.

"If anything detracts you from that relationship, that activity is not from God. God will not ask you to do something that hinders your relationship with Christ. At times, serving God and carrying out His mission is the best way to know and experience God. At other times, it is more important to sit quietly at His feet and listen to what He is saying."

—Henry Blackaby11

"Don't you realize it's the doing that often gets us into trouble? It's not the doing that makes God happy. It's not about what we've done . . . it's about what been done for us."

—Tricia Goyer and Ocieanna Fleiss,
Love Finds You in Glacier Bay, Alaska

Four Keys to Fast Writing {For Writer Moms}

Some people call me a speed-writer. Maybe I am. One reason that I'm able to write "fast" is because I have a lot of practice. I've been writing since 1994, and I write most days except Sunday. There are days I don't write, but most days I do. There are also days I write FAR longer than three hours. So, if I were to be conservative and say that I wrote three hours a day for nineteen years (excluding Sundays), that's 17,841 hours of writing! What could you accomplish if you had 17,000 HOURS of practice?

In life, there are many things we can focus on and learn to be fast at. I have friends who can read fast—they read two to three books a day. I have friends who can cook fast, clean fast, or paint artwork fast. There are times I'm envious of their skill, but I also tell myself that if I were to put my time, attention, and focus into the same things I could be fast too.

Fast writing starts with DEDICATION. It's about setting your mind on something and working at it even if it doesn't seem like you're succeeding. When I first started writing I got lots of rejection letters. If I were to kept them I'd have hundreds and hundreds of rejections. But because I was dedicated to my writing, I did it a lot, even when I didn't succeed. Eventually I started succeeding, and as I continued to practice my craft it got easier and the writing got faster. Fast writing is centered on FAITH. The hardest part about writing is staring at the blank page. Fifteen minutes ago I stared at a blank page and wondered what I wanted to talk to all of you about, but I sent up a quick prayer and then I started to think about what I had to share about my

job as a writer.

Just thirty minutes ago I was chatting with my pastor on the phone and he mentioned, "You write so fast." I put two and two together, and this segment emerged. My pastor's a great writer too, and I guarantee the more time he puts into it the faster he'll get. (Hear that, Harry Li?)

The faith part is centered on the fact that even if the words aren't all figured out in your mind, they will make sense on the page as you work through them. It's trusting that if God has given you something to say He will help you to get it out. Sometimes your skill needs to catch up with your passion, but if it's a message God wants you to share, then it's worth practicing and honing your skills.

I can't tell you how many times I sit down to write an article or a novel and wonder what I even have to say. Faith is knowing that God will show up as I move my fingers over the keyboards . . . and He always does.

Also, you can't have fast writing without FOCUS. This one is hardest for me. There are always emails to answer, laundry to be done, toys to be picked up, phone calls to return, and exercise to fit in. Fast writing happens when the television is off, the email is ignored, the laundry sits piled up, and my mind is on the task at hand.

If you're waiting to get your schedule cleared so you can write, I guarantee it will never happen. If you're comparing your skill today with someone who's written for at least 17,000 hours, then you'll never finish anything. Instead, you must focus on the words on the page and who you are AT THAT MOMENT. The moment will pass whether you're working on your novel or folding laundry, and I guarantee you will become the writer you want to be if you take time to focus again, and again, and again.

Finally, fast writing happens when you FREE YOURSELF UP inside. If you are worried or stressed—or are still carrying around burdens from past sins—you're not going to be free to let your fingers fly.

Freedom comes from forgiveness. Have you taken time to get right with God, to accept His forgiveness, and to forgive yourself? If not, that's something you need to go to God about.

Freedom inside allows the words to flow. Freedom lets your life flow easier too. God is waiting there. Waiting for you to open yourself up to Him. You can't run if you're burdened down, which means I write "fast" because I've taken my burdens to God. I've allowed Him to heal me, and I've been amazed by the change.

TRUE FREEDOM

This last point may not seem to fit with the others, but stay with me for a bit. I wrote for years and years without any success, but when I let God work on the inside it was amazing how everything changed on the outside. As I walk in freedom, the words come freely. As I write in freedom, I allow God to speak through me onto the page.

I never meant to end on this point. I simply thought this chapter was going to talk about "sitting there and doing the hard work." But sometimes the hardest work is dealing with our spiritual selves. I never would have been able to spend 17,000 hours on anything if I was still carrying around the pain, burdens, and heartache of my past.

Want to be fast? First be free, and only the redeeming power of Jesus can do that work in you. Let Him! Then be determined, have faith, make yourself focus, and let His freedom fill your soul, your life, and your words!

Understand Your Life and Family Themes

Another way to find freedom is to know WHO you are. There are times I've tried to copy other writers and nothing has come from that—only rejection. I write a lot now. I write novels, non-fiction books, blogs, children's books, books for teens, books for moms, you name it. And while this seems scattered for most people, every book I write is an extension of my core. How do I know this? Throughout the years I've come to understand my eight life and family themes.

Why eight? A list of eight gives you enough space to express what's inside you, but it's not too much to scatter your intentions.

In Hebrew, the number eight is Sh'moneh, from the root Shah'meyn, "to make fat," "cover with fat," and "to super- abound." As a participle, it means "one who abounds in strength," etc.

When you can sum up who you are simply and accurately in eight points, you can abound with strength and passion.

I have many interests, so it took some time to figure out my core. These are the themes I came up with. These are themes I write about, but more than that, they are themes I live.

Eight things to write about life themes:
- Hope beyond unplanned pregnancy
- Following God's dreams for your life

- Being shaped by God in your role as a wife and parent
- Stepping out of yourself to impact your community and world
- Mentoring
- Replacing lies with truth
- Finding hope in God's Promises (His Word)
- Adoption

Because I know the themes of my life, I then have direction for what to focus on. Here are eight focuses I've identified for my family.

Eight family themes focuses:

- Family meals establish patterns of health, family togetherness, and community .
- Family service to be ambassadors of Christ . As our children see us serve others they see what our faith means to us doing missions work in the Czech Republic, volunteering at a pregnancy center, and attending a multi-ethnic church .

• The foundation of God's Word—putting God's Word deep in our hearts builds a foundation that lasts a lifetime . We accomplish this through children's church, homeschooling, and the example we set when they see us doing our own personal study .

• The power of story—there's nothing like a story to ignite the imagination, so we spend a lot of time reading at night, writing, and communicating in story .

• Mentoring, walking alongside those in personal relationships and encouraging our children to do the same, is important to us too . It's the same thing Jesus did with His disciples .

• Friends matter! We seek healthy community for our kids through sports and other activities .

• Traveling allows us to enjoy God's world and each other .

• Adoption, and opening our home to the elderly, emotionally needy, and orphans is foundational to our faith . James 1:27 (NIV) says, "Religion that God our Father accepts as pure and faultless is this: to look after orphans and widows in their distress and to keep oneself from being polluted by the world ."

EIGHT

I love sharing the idea of "eight" at conferences because I see the lights going on around the room as I talk. Discovering our life themes help us to determine our life's purpose. And knowing our life's purpose helps us determine our goals. And once we determine our goals, we'll have guidance for planning our days.

Another cool thing is the number eight, turned on its side, is the symbol for infinity. It is a reminder of God's presence in our life themes. According to wikipedia.org, "Infinity is an abstract concept describing something without any limit and is relevant in a number of fields, predominately mathematics and physics. The English word infinity derives from Latin infinitas, which can be translated as 'unboundedness,' itself calqued from the Greek word apeiros, meaning 'endless.'"12

When you discover your life themes, you aren't limiting yourself. Instead you're understanding who God made you to be—and the purpose He designed for you. God is the "unboundedness" part of the equation. You + Him = endless possibilities of impacting the world for His glory.

So how do you determine these themes?

Theme-Finding

"All great books come from the heart of the author and from the essence of the author's life experiences," says my friend and fellow author Robin Jones Gunn. I believe this goes beyond writing. All great work comes from our heart and the essence of our life experiences. When you pay attention to the high spots and low points of your life, you'll discover it was in those places that God did the most work.

Two questions Robin encouraged me to ask myself were:

- What purpose has He given me?
- What is His desire?

To flesh this out, Robin encouraged me write out my personal story, starting from my birth to present day–writing out those high and low points—paying attention to the following key elements:

- Key people who helped shape my choices or influenced me
- Key events, some of which I had control over and others I had no control over
- Key lessons I learned along the way
- Key lies I and others told myself, some of which I still believe and need to cast off

This was a life-transforming activity, and these themes could clearly be seen in my life. When you sit down to do this you'll be amazed by how God has been at work in these themes in your life even before you were old enough to realize it! When we focus on eternity and who God has designed us to be, we will truly understand the core of ourselves. And it's from this place that our truest work and service to our family will emerge.

Pause and Reflect

What do you want to ensure lasts for eternity? Where has God directed your service?

What are your eight life themes? What are your eight family focuses?

Tips from the Trenches

"In 1992 I was the mother of four children, aged eleven, twelve, fourteen, and sixteen, and in August we buried our five-year-old son after many struggles with various illnesses. That same month we went through a horrific church split in a community that was so interconnected that father was truly turned against son and brother against brother. We lost two dear friends who got caught up in the us versus them—my husband and I being the them. We started building a new house in three months because we had to get out of our old one by December 1.

"Through all this I continued to write a humor column for three newspapers and had my romance novel rejected by Harlequin and six other Christian publishers. This made me realize I needed to find a way to write the kind of romance novels I wanted to and stay true to my faith. Love Inspired wasn't even a blip on the radar at that time and no other Christian publisher would accept romance novels, but I kept writing, thinking that somehow, someone would want this book.

"And everything that happened to us became fodder for the stories I still continue to write. Currently I have thirty- six novels behind me and am still carrying on, still writing romance and still loving it."

—Novelist Carolyne Arsen

"I also try to weigh my motives. Am I doing what I'm doing because it's what God desires, or because I'm afraid people will be disappointed if I don't?"
—Tricia Goyer, The Memory Jar

When You Don't Know What to Do

When you don't know what to do . . . what you do speaks volumes.

Do you call others for advice?

Do you Google the question, looking for answers? Do you seek input from a professional?

Do you share your problem, hoping to gain sympathy?

Or do you ask for prayer?

And when you ask for prayer, do you spill out every detail, hoping for advice as a bonus? Or do you ask simply, knowing God already knows the issue?

Do you pay attention to the messages God sends to you? (For me they seem to pop up in books, in conversations, and in memories.)

Do you contemplate where God has been leading you up to this point?

Do you read His Word?

Do you listen to His still, small voice?

Do you weigh the thoughts that enter your mind, putting them on a scale and deciphering lies from truth?

Do you let worries lead you down every dark path? Do you talk through your concerns with those who have a stake in your decision, seeking advice?

Do you listen? Really listen to the concerns of others?

Do you worry about your comfort, your image, or your pride?

Or do you ask God to push you out of your comfort zone so He can be glorified?

Do you step back so God can show up?

Do you get on your knees and open up your heart to Him?

When you don't know what to do . . . You can do something.

You can worry and wait. Or you can wait and seek.

You can seek . . . and wait for the peace of God to come.

God's direction may lead to complete dependence on Him. (It most likely will.)

God's plan will be foolish to many (because of their own worries and concerns about how your decision will impact them . . . or compassionate worries for your welfare).

God's plan is rooted in love—for your family, for your community, for your world, and, yes, for you. God's peace will make your roots grow deep in Him as He guides your decision.

God's love will be displayed as your walk of faith is watched.

God's joy will come in unexpected times and in unexpected ways.

When you don't know what to do . . .

Turn to the One who has the right answer. Turn to the One who is the right answer.

If what you do speaks volumes, what He does fills the expanse of the sky.

God's way is the one you'd choose if you knew everything (and loved completely) as He does.

I promise.

Something to Think About

"Take a good look, friends, at who you were when you got called into this life. I don't see many of 'the brightest and the best' among you, not many influential, not many from high-society families. Isn't it obvious that God deliberately chose men and women that the culture overlooks and exploits and abuses, chose these 'nobodies' to expose the hollow pretensions of the 'somebodies'? That makes it quite clear that none of you can get by with blowing your own horn before God. Everything that we have—right thinking and right living, a clean slate and a fresh start—comes from God by way of Jesus Christ.

That's why we have the saying, 'If you're going to blow a horn, blow a trumpet for God,'"

—1 Corinthians 1:26–31 (The Message).

Tips from the Trenches

"Wherever you are in your day, be present. When you're writing, be fully there. When you're with your kids, be fully there."

"You must allow the Holy Spirit to guide you daily to know how to invest your time and effort. Each day may not be lived with perfect balance, but at the close of your life, you will discover you have accomplished everything God assigned you to do."

—Henry Blackaby13

Chapter Eleven

Balance Isn't the Ultimate Goal— Knowing God Is

I waited until the end of the book to drop the bombshell.

After all we've talked about, you need to know that balance isn't the ultimate goal.

A quest for balance leads to frustration and exhaustion. I never have a day when I achieve the perfect balance of work, family, God, and friends. It's impossible. There are always interruptions. If we are working with real-life people, we cannot schedule our time as if we were simply sitting at a computer all day.

And even on days when I've gotten a babysitter and planned to have a whole day at the computer, things come up. I get an urgent or important phone call that can't wait. My grandma gets sick. The neighbor needs help. For years I thought of people as interruptions, and I hated when someone tried to push into my time. I still struggle with this, but over and over God speaks to my heart that people are most important.

And even when people leave us alone, life throws us curveballs. The toilet breaks and begins to flood the house just when I sit down to write. (Yes, this has happened.) The thing to tell myself is that God is not surprised by interruptions. He allows them into our day, sometimes for the sake of others and sometimes for the sake of us. He wants us to turn to Him—to know Him.

Jesus Was Not Balanced

"The people we know who have been used by God to dramatically change their world have been noticeably imbalanced. Jesus was not balanced. At one point in his life, he spent forty days fasting and communing with his Father. At other times, he was so pressed upon by the crowds who followed him that to be able to pray he would escape to a mountain, pray through the night or rise up early in the morning (Mark 1:35; 6:46; Luke 6:12). Jesus could share a meal at times

with his disciples (Luke 33:14-33). On other occasions, he would forego eating because he had more important things to do (John 4:32). Jesus would sometimes invite people to come to him to receive rest (Matt. 11:28). At other times, Jesus was so weary, even a life-threatening storm could not rouse him from his slumber (Matt. 8:24-25). "Jesus lived his life with passion but not necessarily with balance. Yet at the close of his life, he concluded, 'I have glorified You on the earth by completing the work You gave Me to do' (John 17:4). Likewise, at his death, Jesus triumphantly cried: 'It is finished!' (John 19:30). What was his secret? He constantly sought his Father's agenda, and his Father consistently showed him what he should do that day (John 5:19-20, 30)."
—Henry Blackaby, Richard Blackaby, God in the Marketplace14

"God created you with special talents for a purpose, and sometimes those we love most don't understand that. Don't let the doubts of others ring louder than God's whispers to your spirit. Sometimes God's whispers are harder to hear, but they're to be trusted the most."

—Tricia Goyer, The Memory Jar

Scheduling Your Work

I am so thankful Jesus gave us a glimpse of what it looks like to obey God, love others, and serve with passion and dedication. It's OK to work hard! It's OK to spend yourself for God's kingdom when He opens the doors and He asks you to walk through.

Being a balanced mom and stay-at-home worker doesn't mean just giving half-effort in both. It's giving full effort in the moment you are focused on that task. And here are some ideas to help you schedule your work:

1. Be realistic about how much time it will take to do a good job on that project. Figure out how much time you need . . . and then double it. There will always be emergencies, kids who don't cooperate, and unproductive days.

2. Figure out the hours you are most productive. I write best when I've had quiet time with God and my heart is full-to-overflowing, yet this is also the time my children start waking up and needing my attention. Sometimes I schedule my quiet time later in the day. Or sometimes I wake up EVEN earlier. I also work well after the kids go to bed, but usually nap time in the afternoons doesn't work for me. I'm just as sluggish as the kids!

3. If possible, schedule office hours. It's impossible for me to create a set weekly schedule. I don't always work Monday, Wednesday, and Friday from noon to four (or whatever schedule that would be). My schedule is flexible depending on what appointments or therapy my kids have, but during those hours I know it's work time. When I'm done, I'm done. I let my little ones know ahead of time that Mom is working, and I give them a general time frame of when I'll be done. For example I may say, "Mom is working on her computer, but by the time you wake up from your nap, my computer will be put away and

we'll have time to play." Then, I'll do my best to stick to my promise!

4. Find a parenting helper. During my work time I often have my kids out of the house, but sometimes I'll have someone come to my house. Currently a young woman named Holly watches my kids while I write. She also does simple chores like loading the dishwasher and putting away a few loads of laundry, which is a huge help!

5. Set a schedule within a schedule. I often break up my work hours into manageable chunks. I've trained myself to be able to concentrate for thirty-to-fifty minutes at a stretch, but anything more than that drains me—I soon find my mind wandering. So I write for fifty minutes, then answer emails for thirty, etc.

6. I give myself word count/project goals or a time goal, and then I set to work. When the task or time is done, I can check email, get up and stretch, or switch to another task.

7. I schedule the hardest tasks first. I don't like packaging books to mail, and I don't like phone calls,

so I do these first. There are also writing projects that are harder than others. Once I get those things marked off my list, the rest come easy!

8. Don't let the chatter distract you. I ignore most phone calls during my work hours. I turn off Facebook and Twitter. Many things want to pull my attention away, so I choose to mute the noise in order to focus on the project.

9. Say yes to your family. Just as you schedule in work time, make sure to schedule in fun family time. Your husband and kids have an easier time letting you concentrate on your work knowing their time is coming up. I also like to reward my family when I finish a project with a new family game, dinner out, or a fun activity. They are part of why I'm able to do what I do, and I want them to reap the rewards.

Clearing out Your Inner Clutter

It's not just the outer stuff that hinders us, but the inner stuff too. It's the worries and the concerns. It's the lists that scroll through your mind of things that need to get done. Here are more ways to clear your inner clutter.

10.   Make a list of everything holding you back. How many of them are tangible issues you need to address? How many of them are fears or worries that may or may not transpire? Once they're written out, hand them over to God by putting them in a prayer box—they're His now. Picture them in His hands.

11. If things aren't going right with a work project, ask yourself, "What is the worst-case scenario here?" For me one worst-case scenario was having to ask an editor for more time for a project (which has happened to me). Yet even worse than this is NOT accepting a project I feel God wants me to take, not rising to the challenge, not depending on God, and not modeling to my kids what following His dreams in faith looks like.

12. When it comes to ANY kind of writing, the first thing I do is just start writing. You'll be amazed at how that inner storehouse magically fills up the page. Seriously, I open up a blank document and

"clear out" my mind. Today, I did this for a new book I want to write. This morning I had nothing, and this afternoon I had enough of the idea down to email a basic outline to my agent. For me, the best way to deal with a blank page is to make it un- blank.

13. I don't know about you, but all the chores I have to do clutter my mind and spirit too. One of the smartest things I've ever done is training my kids to help around the house. Even before my oldest son could read, he'd used the washing machine with the help of a little angel sticker on the dial to show him where to start. Not only does this help me, but my kids have pride in their work . . . and they'll make good spouses some day! (I'm taking applications for my yet-unmarried kids!)

14. It's important for me to submit to the Prince of Peace. Every day I start my day by reading my Bible and praying. What a difference it makes! As I turn my thoughts to God and submit my will, my steps follow Him and not my own desires. When I turn to Jesus, peace comes.

"There are two great days in our lives. The day we were born, and the day we discovered why."
—William Barclay

"When I've complained to the Lord about not enough time, I think I hear His whisper, 'You have plenty of time to do what I've called you to do. It's the things you do on your own that gum up the works.'"
—Writer Jeanette Levellie

24 Final Tips

I want to leave you with some last parting thoughts. When you are stuck in your work-at-home-ness, here's some good advice you can come back to over and over again:

1. Remember, you can do more than you think.
2. Turn off Twitter and Facebook.
3. Turn off the television.
4. You can't multi-task. Every one minute of interruption is a loss of more than one minute of work. It takes a while to get your mind to focus again.

5. Cut anything out of your schedule you're only doing because you feel guilty.

6. Cut out anything you're doing because you feel you should do it, not because you want to do it.

7. Schedule all of your errands to one day a week.

8. Use the Crock-Pot more.

9. Let your house be dirtier than you normally would. (You'll survive, I promise!)

10. Life doesn't have to be crazy-busy. Just because the people around you are trying to do it all doesn't mean you have to. Just do the things God's shown you to do.

11. Don't give yourself an excuse to put your calling or passion to the side with, "When the kids start school," or, "When the children are out of the house," or some other excuse. If God is calling you to start, then just do it.

12 . Work takes time, and time isn't free. You have to pay for it. You have to buy it by cutting out other things. Make sure your work is worth the cost.

13. As one person you can only do so much.

14. You are your kids' only mom.

15. You are your husband's only wife.

16. Work in spurts.

17. Remember you are an example in life even more than in words. Your life validates your words.

18. Write something worth living for or live in a way that's worthy to write about. (Benjamin Franklin said that.)

19. When you first start working at home, don't depend on your income to pay the basic bills.

20. Don't spend the work money before you get it.

21. Listen to your husband and good friends' advice.

22. If someone thinks you are taking on too much, listen to them.

23. If you don't feel comfortable about something, listen to that inner nudge, even if you're afraid you're going to miss a good opportunity.

24. Finally ask, "Is fear or is peace guiding my choice?" Go with peace. That is where Jesus is. Trust that.

Parting Advice

As an author I always have the feeling I can do more, give more, and say more, but there comes the time I must turn my work over to the reader. It's then that their work begins

. . . and that's especially true for this book.

I want you to know a few things before we part. First, I believe in you. I know God has a good plan for your life and for your kids' lives. I'm proud you're taking the effort to read books like this. It shows your dedication right there!

I also want you to know that God has even better advice than I can give. He's far, far smarter. I love connecting on Facebook, Twitter, my blogs, and through email, so feel free to connect with me! I'd love it! But also know I won't have all the answers for your situation. I can't help everyone—as much as I'd like to!—but the great thing is that God is there. Turn to Him. Seek Him. Read His Word. Listen to His Spirit. God has a good plan for you, friend: for you, your work, and your family. And when others ask how you do it all . . . just think of all the good news of Jesus you'll have to share!

To God be the glory!

Want more balance in your life?

Want more balance in your life? Head to Tricia's website (www.triciagoyer.com/how-to-balance/) for more resources, printables, and advice on balancing career, mommyhood, and your relationship with God.

About the Author

Tricia Goyer is a busy mom of ten, grandmother of many, and wife to John. Somewhere around the hustle and bustle of family life, she manages to find the time to write fictional tales delighting and entertaining readers and non-fiction titles offering encouragement and hope.

A bestselling author, Tricia has published forty books to date and has written more than 500 articles. She is a two time Carol Award winner, as well as a Christy and ECPA Award Nominee. In 2010, she was selected as one of the Top 20 Moms to Follow on Twitter by SheKnows.com. Tricia is also on the blogging team at MomLifeToday.com, TheBetterMom.com and other homeschooling and Christian sites. In addition to her roles as mom, wife and author, Tricia volunteers around her community and mentors teen moms. She is the founder of Hope Pregnancy Ministries in Northwestern Montana, and she currently leads a Teen MOPS Group in Little Rock, AR.

Learn more about Tricia at www.triciagoyer.com, or connect with her on these social media platforms:

Facebook: www.facebook.com/authortriciagoyer

Twitter: www.twitter.com/triciagoyer

Pinterest: www.pinterest.com/triciagoyer

Instagram: http://instagram.com/triciagoyer

References

1 Bailey, Becky, I Love You Rituals, 2000, New York, NY, HarperCollins Publisher Inc., p. 26

2 Blackaby, Henry, Chosen to Be God's Prophet, 2003, Nashville, Tennessee, Thomas Nelson Publishers, p. 4-5

3 Horn, Sara, "That's Intriguing #95: What Can Ukulele Player Jake Shimabukuro Teach Us about Communication?" The Intrigue Agency, May 11, 2013, Article was accessed November 5, 2013 http://samhornpop.wordpress.com/2013/05/11/thats-intriguing-95-what-can-ukulele-player-jake-shimabukuro-teach-us-about-communication/

4 Ken Blanchard, Phil Hodges, Tricia Goyer, Lead Your Family Like Jesus, 2013, Carol Stream, Illinois, Tyndale House Publisher, Inc. p. 38-39

5 Alina Tugend, Family Happiness and the Overbooked Child, The New York Times, published August 12, 2011, Accessed November 5, 2013 http://www.nytimes.

com/2011/08/13/your-money/childrens-activities-no-guarantee-of-later-success.html?pagewanted=all&_r=0

6 Wikipedia.org "Colosseum", Wikipedia Foundation Inc, This page was last modified on 7 September at 11:50, Article was accessed November 5, 2013 http://en.wikipedia.org/wiki/Colosseum

7 Leslie Vernick, How to Act Right When Your Spouse Acts Wrong (Colorado Springs: WaterBrook, 2001), 112-113.

8 Dennis & Barbara Rainey, Staying Close (Nashville, Tennessee: Thomas Nelson Publishers, 2003) p. 87

9 Marshall, Peter, Mr. Jones Meet the Master, Grand Rapids, MI, Fleming H. Revell, Co, 1950, p. 55

10 Bailey, Becky, I Love You Rituals, 2000, New York, NY, HarperCollins Publisher Inc., p. 20

11Blackaby, Henry, Experiencing God, Day by Day, Nashville, Tennesse, B&H Publishing Group, p 337-338

12 Wikipedia.org "Infinity" http://en.wikipedia.org/wiki/ Infinity, Wikipedia

Foundation Inc, This page was last modified on 27 October 2013 at 10:20, Article was accessed November 5, 2013

13 Blackaby, Henry, God in the Marketplace: 45 Questions Fortune 500 Executives Ask About Faith, Nashville, Tennessee, B&H Publishing Group, p. 170

14 Blackaby, Henry. Blackaby, Richard, God in the Marketplace: 45 Questions Fortune 500 Executives Ask About Faith, Life and Business, Nashville, Tennessee, B&H Publishing Group, p. 169-170

Made in the USA
Columbia, SC
19 April 2024

34304507R00117